PETER BISH

INTRODUCING INFORMATION TECHNOLOGY

Nelson

Thomas Nelson and Sons Ltd
Nelson House   Mayfield Road
Walton-on-Thames   Surrey
KT12 5PL   UK

51 York Place
Edinburgh
EH1 3JD   UK

Thomas Nelson (Hong Kong) Ltd
Toppan Building 10/F
22A Westlands Road
Quarry Bay   Hong Kong

Distributed in Australia by

Thomas Nelson Australia
480 La Trobe Street
Melbourne   Victoria 3000
and in Sydney, Brisbane, Adelaide and Perth

© P. Bishop 1987
First published by Thomas Nelson and Sons Ltd 1987
ISBN 0-17-448137-3
NPN 01
Printed in Great Britain by M. & A. Thomson Litho Ltd

Preface

• Everyone needs to know something about Information Technology. The need is not for technical knowledge of how computer systems work, but practical knowledge, and a certain amount of 'hands-on' experience, of how they are used. It is also essential to appreciate why Information Technology is used, how it is finding a place in almost every type of work, and some of the consequences of its introduction. These are important skills for everyone, and relate closely to other skills such as organising information, making decisions, solving problems – and using language to communicate these processes.

This is the motivation behind the introductory Information Technology courses for which **Do IT!** is intended. The aims of the book are as follows:

• To form the course text for introductory Information Technology courses for school pupils aged 11 to 13 years.

• To introduce the use of computers, electronic communications and control systems as tools for information management, via a representative range of IT-related activities.

• To introduce, and to develop through practical experience, the skills of information management – designing information structures; collecting, manipulating and presenting information; drawing conclusions.

• To provide a resource of knowledge and skills which can be used throughout the secondary school curriculum, as IT becomes an accepted tool in a range of subjects.

The book is also suitable for the RSA **Computer Literacy and Information Technology (CLAIT)** course.

Do IT! is built around a series of **activites**, each covering an essential area of IT in practice: word processing, information storage and retrieval, spreadsheets, stock control, computer-aided design, processing tables of numbers, viewdata, electronic mail and electronic control systems. At the start of the book is a general introduction to information and the key elements of information technology: computers, communications and control systems. At the end of the book is a general conclusion which draws together the threads.

Each activity is introduced by two contrasting stories – one describing how things are (or were) done before the advent of IT, and the other telling it like it is today. The essential concepts of the activity are stated, briefly and clearly. Then follows a series of suggestions for activities using the software now available in schools, which mirrors the practice in commerce and industry. The key computer elements which are emphasised in the particular activity are then described. There is a concluding section discussing the activity in practice, and some of its implications. Each section is followed by a set of comprehension questions, and there is a graded exercise at the end of each chapter.

Do IT! is intended to be used in conjunction with a number of software items, but is not directly linked to any particular computer or software package. In most cases the school will already have the hardware and software needed, but a list of suitable items, and some guidance about their use, is included in a separate Teacher's Book.

Do IT! is a book about the modern world, and the place of Information Technology in the modern world. It is a world in which decisions must be made, deadlines must be met, costs must be controlled – and all work must be done to the very highest standards possible. It is a world in which people use Information Technology to do their jobs more effectively. **Do IT!** aims to open pupils' eyes to this world, to enable them to sample it, discuss it and think about it from the security of the classroom, so that, when the time comes, they are ready to face it themselves.

Disclaimer

This book contains a number of stories which are intended to be as realistic as possible. They are not, however, literally true. Any resemblance between the people, companies and events described in these stories and actual people, companies and events is entirely coincidental.

Acknowledgements

A number of people have been of great help in formulating the concept of this book, planning it and reviewing the plans, supplying source material, and reviewing the various drafts. My thanks go in particular to John Anderson (Information Technology Inspector, Northern Ireland), Andrew Terry (Prestel), Michael Smith (Computing Adviser, Sandwell), David Thomson (Microelectronics Adviser, Sandwell), and Philip Hepburn (Computing Adviser, Gwent) for their time and expertise. I am grateful to David Futcher (Educational Computing) for his help in preparing the list of recommended software. The passages in French were translated by Jöelle Plumerel (Christ's School, Richmond). Much of the administrative work and checking of drafts was done by Sarah Bishop. The text of the book was prepared on a Research Machines Nimbus Microcomputer using the WordStar word processing system.

Peter Bishop

19th September 1986

Contents

CHAPTER 1

Introduction

● An air traffic controller has three aircraft on his radar screen. He is directing them all towards the same place, where they will turn to come into land. He must decide which plane will be first, and which of the others will follow it. The weather is very bad, and the pilots of the aircraft cannot see each other. All three have come from a long way away, and none has very much fuel left. He does not have much time to decide...

● An oil company is deciding whether or not to drill a new well in the North Sea. It will cost tens of millions of pounds. The well may find large quantities of oil, or none at all. The company has to take into account many factors. These include changes in the price of oil and in the demand for oil. Changes in the values of the currencies in which oil is bought and sold must also be considered. A wrong decision could put the company out of business...

● The police are called to the scene of a murder. They photograph the body, take fingerprints at the scene and start looking for clues. They search the surrounding area, and question all the people living in nearby houses. The amount of information they gather increases very quickly. They create files to store the information, and classify it into categories. They compare the information about this murder with that about previous murders...

● A small company has just developed a new type of disco lighting. The marketing manager of the company wants to tell its customers about the new product. She has a list of all the customers, which includes information about the lighting they have bought in the past. She has composed a letter, telling them about the new lighting system. She wants to send a copy of the letter, personally addressed to each customer, and modified depending on what the customer has bought in the past...

Donna and Blitzen
Lighting Company
33 ALBERT ROAD CAMDEN   LONDON NW3 5PJ

3rd December 1986

Mr Benjamin Frank
Manager
The Boom Town
The Bull Ring
Birmingham   B3 5TY

Dear Ben

Blitz Lighting System

Put on your darkest dark glasses! The Blitz lighting system is here!.

Yes, after two years of development, we are pleased to announce that our Blitz lighting system is complete. Are you ready for it?

Blitz is a totally new concept in disco lighting. It includes searchlights, multiple laser beams and a flash-floodlight that will make you blink ... even with your darkest dark glasses on.

Blitz is computer-controlled. You can set up whatever amazing effects you want beforehand, and either call them up at the touch of a button, or set them to be triggered automatically by the music ... or any combination of these.

I am enclosing a price list and order form. Yes, these are the real prices - much less than any other system available.

Please let me know when you are ready to put on your darkest dark glasses....

Regards

H L'Estrange

Helen L'Estrange
Donna and Blitzen Lighting Company

QUESTIONS

1 What do the stories above have in common?

2 Why is information important in each story?

3 List the types of information mentioned in each story.

4 Write short descriptions of other, similar situations.

1.1 The World of Information

A sundial — an old way of providing information. It is difficult to read and not very accurate.

Everything we do needs information. The stories in the previous section are just a few examples of this. When we make a telephone call, we need to know the number. When we buy a book, we need to know the title and author, and have some idea of the price. When we travel by train, we need to know the train times and fares. When we plan a holiday, we need to find out a lot of information beforehand. If any of the information is wrong, the holiday could be a disaster!

Many years ago, when life was simpler, people did not need so much information. They needed to know when to plant crops, and what food to give their animals. The first traders needed to know where different goods were to be found, and how many of one item could be swapped for one of another item. As societies got more complex, more information was needed. People needed to know the time and the date, distances between towns, prices of goods and many other details.

Today, societies depend on information. Industry, commerce and government create huge amounts of information. When people vote in an election, they supply the information which chooses the next government. Every time something is bought or sold, information is created. Every time someone is born, or someone dies, a record is made. Crimes are solved on the basis of information, in the form of evidence which is used in court.

The flight arrivals board at an airport, giving essential information for travellers. It must be kept up-to-date all the time.

It is important to keep information up-to-date, and to ensure that it is accurate. An out-of-date weather forecast is no use at all. If books cannot be found in a library, the information in them is useless. A company which cannot keep records of the customers which owe it money will soon go out of business.

The information provided in holiday brochures enables people to choose their holidays.

Information is valuable, and some of it is private. The formulae for many chemicals and medicines are kept secret by the companies which make them. Companies which manufacture goods keep some aspects of their processes secret, so that their competitors cannot copy them. People's medical records help doctors to cure illnesses, but are not to be shown to other people.

Over the years, many means of keeping records of information have been used. People made marks in pieces of wood or built piles of stones to record the numbers of sheep or cattle they had. Writing, on clay, bark and finally paper, was for centuries the commonest means of recording information. Some information is recorded in the form of maps and charts. Today, the commonest way of recording information is by computer.

QUESTIONS

1 What are the most important items of information which would be needed by the people in a small village where everyone works on the land?

2 Make a list of some items of information which need to be kept secret.

3 Why is it important to keep information up-to-date?

4 List some ways of recording information **not** mentioned in the text.

1.2 Information and Technology

In each of the stories at the start of the chapter, people have to make decisions on the basis of information. The decisions are all important, and have to be made quickly. In most of the situations, there is a lot of information. Some of it is reliable; some is not.

In almost every situation like those in the stories, **technology** is used to deal with the information. **Information technology**, or **IT** for short, includes:

- **computers** which store and process information;

- **communications** networks which send it from one place to another;

- **robots** and devices which **control** equipment automatically.

Computers, communications networks and control systems are all made from **microchips**. Microchips are very small, and have no moving parts. They use small amounts of electricity to store or process information, or send out control signals.

Powerful processing chips used in large mainframe computers. The dark shapes on the top are for cooling.

A BBC Master series microcomputer, used in many schools.

Information technology helps people in many ways. It assists in making decisions, as in the stories above. People use computers to help them plan their work. Computers are used to design goods, and robots to manufacture them. Computers and communications systems are used for all types of business transaction – buying things, booking holidays, cashing cheques. Computers do the difficult calculations needed for scientific experiments and weather forecasting.

Computers do much of the detailed work by themselves — calculations, storing and sorting information. Robots do routine assembly operations with no direct supervision. Telephone exchanges connect calls automatically. But information technology does not solve problems itself. Problems are solved by the way people manage information, using the technology to help them.

A robot used for automatic maintenance of the underwater parts of oil rigs.

QUESTIONS

1 What types of work can computers be used for?

2 What are computers, communications systems and control devices made from?

3 Can computers solve problems all by themselves?

4 List some ways in which information technology can help people.

5 Look back at the stories at the start of the chapter. For each story, state how computers, communications or control equipment are being used to help.

A radio dish which sends telephone and other signals to a satellite, and receives other signals back from the satellite.

1.3 Managing Information

In the stories at the start of this chapter, and in many similar situations, success or failure depends on what is done with the available information. The technology handles the information, but it is up to a person to decide what to do with it. The person has the task of **managing information**.

The aim of this book is to introduce you to the skills of managing information, and to give you some practice in their use. The skills include:

- deciding what information is needed for a particular task;
- collecting information;
- processing information in various ways;
- presenting information as clearly as possible;
- making decisions on the basis of information.

Computers, telecommunications and control systems are used to help you in these tasks, but they will not do them for you!

The ability to manage information helps you in many ways. It helps you to organise your work at school. It helps you to make the best use of your pocket money. The skills of managing information are essential when you leave school or college and start work. They are needed for all types of work, whether you use information technology or not.

For example, suppose that you want to decide the best way of spending your pocket money. Using the ideas of managing information, you could:

- make a list of all the things that you would like to buy;

- find out how much each item costs;

- cross off those that you will never afford!

- divide the list into the items which you can afford with one week's money, and those you have to save up for;

- decide which items are most important, and which can wait;

- plan which items to buy each week, and how much to save, over the next few weeks.

QUESTIONS

1 List some school activities in which you already have to manage information. In what ways can the skills of managing information help you in these activities?

2 Why is it important to learn how to manage information?

3 What methods, apart from information technology, do you already use to help you to manage information? (One answer is pencil and paper.)

4 Suggest some other activities where the skills of managing information can help you. Choose **one** of these, and write down the steps you might use to go about the task, using the ideas of managing information. Use the steps for planning how to spend pocket money as an example.

1.4 Computers

At present the commonest method of storing and processing information is by **computer**. Computers come in all shapes and sizes, but most of them look like the one shown in Figure 1.1. Computers of this type are used in many factories and offices, and most schools have a number of them.

The simplest way of describing a computer is as an **information processing machine**. In fact, a computer can do seven types of tasks:

- Receive **input** information from the person using the computer. The commonest method of input is by typing at a keyboard.

- Supply **output** information to the person using the computer. Computers display output on a screen, and most can print it.

- **Store** large quantities of information on magnetic disks. The information stays permanently on the disk until it is changed by the computer.

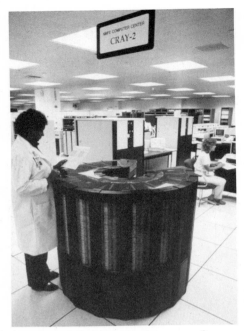

A Cray-2 supercomputer, one of the most powerful computers ever produced.

- **Retrieve** information stored on disk.

- **Send** information to other computers, or devices controlled by the computer. The other computers may be in the same room, or a long way away. Information is sent over long distances by telephone lines.

- **Receive** information from other computers or sensing devices.

- **Process** information in a number of ways. The processing tasks which a computer can perform are quite simple. They include sorting and selecting information, and doing calculations. Computers can make decisions based on the information, and send control signals. But they cannot think for themselves!

Of these seven tasks, three are more important that the rest in understanding how a computer is used. They are **input**, **processing** and **output**. Much of the work of a computer can be described as

$$\text{Input} \rightarrow \text{Processing} \rightarrow \text{Output}$$

For example, if a computer is used to prepare a form list in alphabetical order, the steps are:

Input: Type the names of the pupils in the form.

Processing: Sort the names into alphabetical order.

Output: Print the list in order.

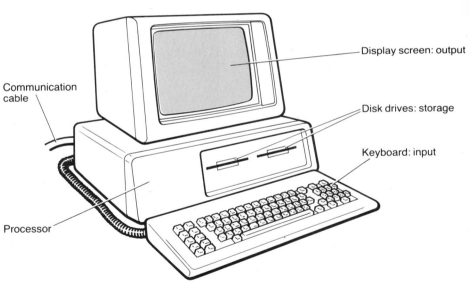

Figure 1.1: The parts of a computer

An RM Nimbus microcomputer, widely used in schools, colleges and businesses.

A portion of the printed circuit board in a digital telephone exchange, showing how the chips are mounted.

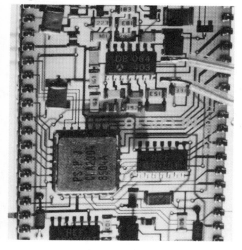

When you use a computer to do a particular task, you load a **program** for the task. A program is a set of instructions which tell the computer how to carry out the steps of the task. You use the keyboard to control the computer, and to enter information. Output is displayed on the screen, or printed. Computer output may be in the form of text, or diagrams. Permanent information is stored on disks, and may be used many times.

If you take off the case of a computer, you will see that it contains a number of **microchips** (or just **chips**) mounted on **printed circuit boards**. The microchips carry out the seven types of operation described above. The most important chip in a computer is the one which does the processing. It is a **microprocessor** chip. The printed circuit board has all the connections between the chips, and is a convenient way of mounting them.

QUESTIONS

1 What is a program?

2 List the **seven** types of processing which a computer can perform. Which **three** are the most important?

3 Look at other photographs of computers. Identify the parts listed in this section.

4 Which chip in a computer does the processing?

5 How are the chips in a computer connected?

1.5 Telecommunications

The commentators at a World Cup football match, each connected via an electronic communications link to their home country.

The **telecommunications** network has grown out of the telephone system. It now connects hundreds of millions of users throughout the world, and carries thousands of millions of calls and messages every day. In addition to carrying telephone calls, it is used for **television** pictures and **telex** messages. It also carries information between computers. As shown in Figure 1.2, it consists of:

- **local lines**, which connect individual telephones and computers to exchanges;

- **exchanges** which switch calls and packets of information;

- **trunk lines** which link exchanges, often over long distances, carrying large numbers of calls.

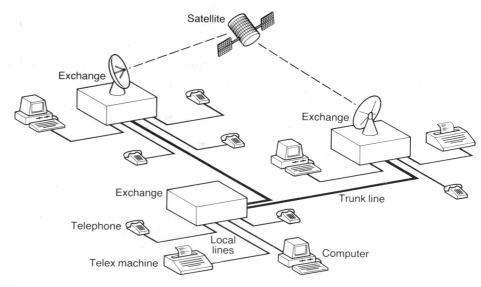

Figure 1.2: Telecommunications network

Two strands of a fibre optics cable, being passed through the eye of a needle.

Trunk lines can be formed by **microwave radio**, **fibre optics** cable, or **satellite** links. Fibre optics cable is made from thin strands of glass. Signals are sent down the strands as pulses of light. Modern exchanges are electronic, and work like computers. Many exchanges can store computer messages if the receiving computer is not ready for it.

The telecommunications system provides links between computers for a number of purposes. One is the exchange of messages, a service known as **electronic mail**. It also enables computers to use central stores of information, such as the **Prestel** system.

Local area networks link the computers in the same building. They enable the computers to share disk drives and printers, and to exchange information (see Figure 1.3). Many schools have their computers on a local area network.

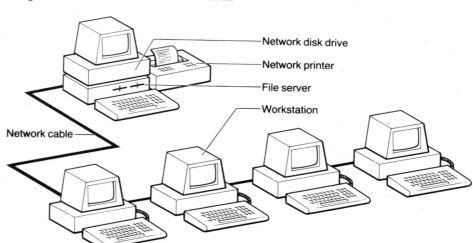

Figure 1.3: Local area network

A computer network in a classroom.

1.6 Control Systems

A Canon camera with microprocessor control, including automatic focusing.

Many items of equipment are controlled automatically. These include robots in factories and automatic washing machines. Most chemical processes such as oil refining are also controlled automatically. Sometimes control is partly automatic. Aircraft landing at most airports are assisted by automatic landing systems — they help to guide the plane in, but the pilot is still in charge. Cars, cameras, video recorders, hi-fi sets and new telephones have some automatic controls.

Figure 1.4 shows the main parts of a **control system**. The main steps of a computing system are input, processing and output. The corresponding steps in a control system are

$$\text{Sense} \rightarrow \text{Decide} \rightarrow \text{Act}$$

In a typical control system, there are **sensors** which take measurements. For example, in an oil refinery, sensors measure the temperature and pressure of the reaction. These measurements are made at regular intervals, in some systems many times a second. Unless control is fully automatic, there is a **control input** from the person operating the system.

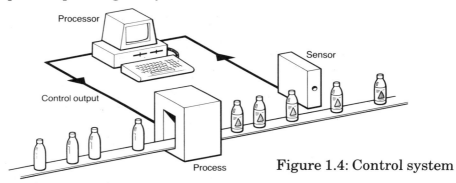

Figure 1.4: Control system

There is a control **processor**, which uses the measurements from the sensors, and the control inputs, to **decide** what control instructions to give. A control processor is either a computer processor, or a special device made from one or more microchips. It is has a **program** which contains the steps which it is to carry out.

The processor issues its instructions via **control outputs**, which are wires connected to the equipment it is controlling. The equipment **acts** in some way in response to the control signals. In an oil refinery, the controls switch on and off the heating elements, and open and close the valves which control the flow of the oil.

On the left is an instrument landing system for aircraft, on the right is a new Plessey microwave landing system which is much more flexible.

QUESTIONS

1 What **two** types of input are there in a control system?

2 An automatic ticket barrier at a station opens when a ticket is inserted. What sensor does it have, and what is its control output?

3 List some devices and processes, other than those mentioned in this section, which are controlled automatically.

1.7 Microchips

Microchips are the key to information technology. Computers, communications networks and control systems are all made from them. They do most of the work of sending, receiving, storing and, above all, processing information.

An IBM experimental memory chip, able to store 256 thousand items of information.

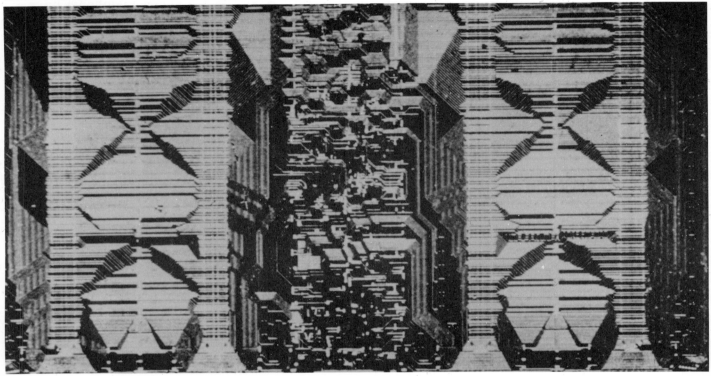

A set of memory chips on the printed circuit board of a computer.

Microchips are very small, but contain thousands of individual components, as shown in the photograph. They use very little electricity while they are working. They will last for many years without breaking down. If they do break down, they are removed and replaced. Most important, they are cheap to produce, and getting cheaper all the time!

The main reason for the very rapid spread of information technology in recent years is the availability of large quantities of cheap, reliable microchips. Microchips which can store more information, or process it more quickly, are being produced all the time. Microchips are being developed for new tasks. For these reasons, new computers are more powerful than old ones, and can do a wider range of tasks. They are also cheaper.

QUESTIONS

1 How reliable are microchips?

2 What is the main reason for the rapid spread of information technology?

3 In what **three** ways do new microchips differ from old ones?

22

Exercise 1

1 Write down the meanings of the following words or phrases: information technology, computer, telecommunications, chip, printed circuit board, input, output, processor, program, trunk line, local area network, sensor.

2 What information do you need to know when you:
a) buy a loaf of bread?
b) buy a train ticket?
c) set off for school in the morning?
d) arrange to meet a friend?
e) choose a birthday present for a friend?

3 There is only one copy of the recipe for Coca Cola, and it is kept in a safe in a bank.
a) Why do you think that this recipe is kept secret?
b) Make a list of some other recipes and formulae which you would expect to be kept secret. For each one, say why you think it should be secret.

4 Decide what types of information are needed for each of the following activities. Say what input is required, how the information is processed and what is the output. Do not give any details. For example:

Activity: Sending appointment reminders at a dentist.

Input: List of names and addresses of patients, dates of last appointments.
Processing: Select all patients whose last appointment was more than six months ago. Copy their names and addresses onto appointment reminder cards.
Output: Set of appointment reminder cards.

Activities —
a) finding where a book is kept in a library;
b) deciding what kind of fridge to buy;
c) planning a meal for group of friends;
d) deciding what price to charge for an item at a shop;
e) making a weather forecast;
f) designing a record cover;
g) using a robot to fit the wheels of a motor car.

5 For each of the above activities, say how IT is being used or could be used.

6 Make a list of all the devices you can think of which contain microchips.

7 Make a list of all the kinds of jobs you can think of where **no** information processing takes place.

Things to Find Out

1 Find out which local firms use computers, what they use them for, and what types of computer they have.

2 Find out whether your local police force uses computers, and, if so, what tasks are done on them.

3 Find out whether computers are used for administration at your school. If so, find out how they are used.

4 Select an item such as a camera, which includes electronic controls. Find out how the price of the item has changed since it was first introduced. Comment on your findings.

Points to Discuss

1 Many devices used in the home are now controlled by microchips. These devices include clocks, vacuum cleaners, washing machines, video recorders, television and hi-fi sets and central heating controls. Discuss the effects these devices are having.

Think about such questions as:

a) Are these devices better than the previous types?
b) What new services have they provided in the home?
c) What changes have they brought about in the home?

2 The worldwide telecommunications network has been built up over the last hundred years. Discuss the benefits it has for:
a) people keeping in touch with their friends;
b) emergency services such as the police and fire brigade;
c) companies in their work.

What benefits do telecommunications have for countries which have problems such as droughts and famines?

CHAPTER 2

Word processing

● Alan Jones dictates a letter to an important client. Jean Preston, his secretary, listens to the tape as she types a **draft** of the letter. She has to stop and rewind the tape several times, and correct the draft with correcting fluid. She takes the draft to Alan.

Alan corrects the draft. Jean retypes the whole letter and gives the **top copy** to Alan to sign. He notices two further errors, which Jean puts right with correcting fluid.

Alan then asks Jean to send two further copies of the letter, with slight changes, to other clients. Jean types these, correcting the mistakes she makes, and Alan signs them. Getting the three letters ready for the post has taken her most of the morning.

● In another company, Susan Maxwell dictates a letter to an important client. Her secretary, Helen Pearce, listens to the tape and enters the letter at her word processor. She corrects the draft on the screen, until she is sure that there are no mistakes. Helen takes the draft to Susan, who checks it and makes a few changes. Helen enters the changes and checks them very carefully on the screen. She prints the top copy of the letter for Susan to sign.

Susan asks for two additional copies of the letter, with some changes, to be sent to other clients. Helen makes two copies of the letter on her disk, and then enters the changes in each copy. She checks them very carefully, making the corrections needed on the screen.

Susan looks at the changes on the screen before Helen prints the top copies. Susan signs them. The three letters are ready for posting in an hour.

QUESTIONS

1 How many times did Jean Preston type the three letters?
How many times did Helen Pearce type them?

Comment on your answers.

2 How did Jean Preston make corrections? Could any corrections be seen on the top copy of the typed letter? How did Helen Pearce make corrections? Could any corrections be seen on the top copy of the letter produced on the word processor?

Comment on your answers.

3 Which method of producing the letters is quicker?

4 Legal documents such as contracts cannot be sent from one company to another unless there are **no** errors in them. If the letters in the stories were legal documents, how would this affect them?

2.1 A Word Processor

An Amstrad PCW 8512, a popular word processor for home and office use.

A word processor is a computer which can be used to type and edit **documents**, save them on disk and print them. (Editing is the process of making corrections, improving the layout of a document, etc.) Documents are letters, articles, chapters of books, contracts, etc. The computer is controlled by a special chip, or a program on disk for word processing.

When typing a new document, the usual steps are:

- open up a new document;
- type the text, making any corrections needed;
- save the document on disk;
- print the document.

When editing an existing document, the steps are:

- call up the document from disk;
- edit the text – make corrections and improve layout, etc.
- save the new version of the document on disk;
- print the document.

(Note that the order of the above steps varies slightly from one word processor to another.)

Each document has a **reference** which identifies it on disk. For example, a letter to David Brown might have the reference **DB8703**, the third letter to David Brown in 1987. When a new document is created, it is given a reference which is different from all the others on the disk. When a document is called up, its reference is used to identify it. Once it has been stored on a disk, a document can be called up, edited and reprinted many times.

When a document is typed or edited, a portion of the text appears on the screen in the same layout as it will appear when printed. There is a **cursor** which can be moved around the screen. The cursor is a bright square or an underline symbol. It shows where the next typed character will appear, or where deleted text will disappear.

Blocks of text may be moved from one place to another in a document. They may be saved separately on disk, and copied into other documents. In this way, sentences, tables and paragraphs can be used in many documents.

QUESTIONS

1 In what ways are typing a new document similar to editing an existing document?

2 What does a cursor do?

3 How is a document identified?

4 How often can an existing document be edited and reprinted?

2.2 Typing a Letter

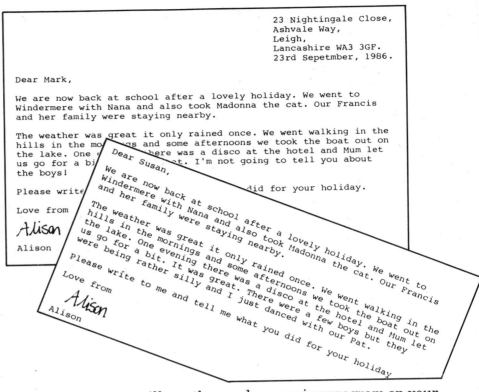

In this section, you will use the word processing program on your school's computer to type a letter to a friend. You will then modify the letter to be sent to another friend.

Run the word processing program on your school's computer. Look at the instructions for the word processing program to find out how to carry out each operation.

- Open up a new document, giving it a suitable reference if necessary at this stage. You should see a blank area on the screen for your letter, with the cursor at the top left.

- Move the cursor over to the right and type the first line of your address.

- Enter the rest of your address and the date on new lines under it.

- Type the text of the letter. Leave a blank line between paragraphs.

- When you have finished, move the cursor back to the top of the letter. Read it carefully on the screen. If you find a mistake, move the cursor to it. Delete the wrong characters and type the correct ones. Then move the text so that left and right margins are lined up.

- When you are quite satisfied with your letter, save it on disk, giving it a suitable reference if it has not already been named. Then print it.

To produce a second copy of the letter, addressed to another friend, make another copy of your letter on the disk. Give the copy a new reference. Use the file copying facility on your computer if the word processor does not have one.

- Call up the copy of the letter and run the cursor through it. Delete the first friend's name, and type the second friend's name. Make any other changes to the letter that you require.

- Check the whole letter carefully, and make any corrections which are necessary. Then save the letter on disk and print it.

QUESTIONS

1 How much extra work would have been needed if you were not using a word processor?

2 Were there any mistakes in the letters that you printed? If so, how could they have been corrected?

3 How easy was it to use the word processor? Comment on your answer.

● **A C T I V I T Y**

2.3 Correcting Errors

```
The Grand Ol Duke of York
He had ten ten thosand men
He marshed them up to the top of the clif
Then he marced them back again.

And when they were up they werre up
Adn where they were down they all down
And when the were only hafway up
They were niether up or douwn.
```

In this section you will use a word processor to correct the mistakes in a piece of text.

- **Either** call up the document on your school's word processor which contains the above text

   or open up a new document and type it (mistakes and all).

- Move the cursor through the document and correct all the mistakes. There are spelling mistakes, grammatical mistakes and wrong words. If necessary, move the text so that there are no gaps.

- When you have corrected all the mistakes, save the correct version of the text and print it.

QUESTIONS

1 How difficult is it to correct mistakes on a word processor?

2 Did you make any more mistakes while correcting the existing ones? Comment on your answer.

3 Can the word processor make any of the corrections by itself?

2.4 Class Newspaper

Most newspapers are produced with the help of word processors. The word processors are linked in a **network**. This allows articles to be passed from one word processor to another. Articles are stored on large central disks. The word processors are linked to other programs which make up the pages of the newspaper, ready to be printed. The reporters enter their stories on the word processors. The editors modify them to fit the space available, and to follow the style of the newspaper. The pages are then made up on a special computer which can display the text of an entire page on its screen. Headings and photographs are placed in the page, which is then sent to be printed.

In this section, a group of between six and twelve pupils will produce a class newspaper using word processors. The word processors must be able to share documents, either on a network, or by passing disks from one to another. This activity may form the basis of an extended project if several issues of the newspaper are produced, or a magazine is produced instead of a newspaper.

First of all, decide on the type of newspaper or magazine to be produced. It may be for school events and news only: sports reports, school trips, interviews with pupils and staff, and advertisements for forthcoming events, lost property, things for sale, etc. It may be for local news and events, or for summaries of world news. Decide how often the newspaper or magazine is to be produced.

Then divide the group into reporters, editors and designers:

- The **reporters** gather the news in their notebooks. They enter their stories at the word processor, using suitable references for the documents.

A reporter typing a story at a word processor terminal.

- The **editors** then call up the stories and edit them. They correct any errors in the stories, and make sure that the style of writing is suitable. They decide which stories are going to be on which pages, and how much space is needed for each.

- The **designers** – *either* print drafts of the edited stories and lay them out on the pages of the newspaper. They leave space for headings, photographs and drawings. If any articles do not fit, they are shortened or lengthened and reprinted. The final versions of the articles are pasted onto the pages. The photographs and drawings are inserted, and the headings written in large letters

  – or they use a page makeup program to produce the pages. They decide on the layout of each page. Pictures and drawings are brought in from copies already on disk. Articles are loaded from the word processor documents into their positions on the page. Headings are set, in whichever size of type is required. When a complete page is ready, a master copy is printed.

The newspaper is now ready to be printed!

QUESTIONS

1 When a newspaper is produced using word processors, how often is each article typed?

2 Do all the word processors used by a newspaper all have to be in the same building? If not, how can they communicate?

3 What are the benefits of newspaper production using word processors?

2.5 Computer Elements: Keyboard, Screen and Printer

The **keyboard** of a computer or word processor is used to type information for the computer to use. There are keys for **letters**, laid out like those on an ordinary typewriter. There is often a separate group of **number** keys, laid out like the keys on a calculator.

There are also **function** keys which are used to perform certain tasks. For example, on many word processors, pressing a function key will move the text in a paragraph to line up the margins. Most

The keyboard of an RM Nimbus microcomputer. The function keys are on the left, the arrow keys on the right.

29

computers have **arrow keys** to move the cursor in the required direction. For example, to move the cursor left, the left arrow key is pressed.

Computers and word processors have a **display screen**, like a television screen, on which the information being processed by the computer appears. In the case of a word processor, this information is the text of the document being typed. Some display screens can show **graphics** (diagrams, graphs, etc.) as well as text.

The **printers** attached to computers and word processors produce **hard copies** of the information processed by the computer. Some can print in several styles, such as *italic* and **bold**, and can vary the size of letters. A few types of printer can print graphics as well as text. Printers work much more slowly than other parts of a computer, and are sometimes rather noisy.

QUESTIONS

1 What **four** kinds of keys are found on computer keyboards?

2 What is the slowest part of a computer?

3 What does the display screen of a word processor show?

2.6 Word Processing in Practice

Word processing is one of the most popular uses of computers. Word processors are steadily taking over from typewriters in offices. Companies of all sizes are finding that word processors are faster,

Office computers, used for word processing and other tasks.

A Toshiba portable computer, battery-powered, which can be used for a range of tasks.

more flexible and produce work of a much higher standard than typewriters. In many companies, word processing is linked to other uses of computers. Text can be transferred from the other applications to the word processor, without having to be retyped. For example, a table of figures produced by another program can be transferred into a report produced by a word processor.

Portable computers and word processors are now available. These enable people to use them at home or at work, or even when travelling by train or aircraft. This allows people to work more flexible hours, and to work while they are travelling. Word processors at home enable mothers with young children to continue working.

QUESTIONS

1 How popular are word processors in business?

2 Are word processors only used in the office?

3 Why are word processors taking over from typewriters?

4 List some of the effects of the use of word processors.

Exercise 2

1 Write down the meanings of the following words or phrases: word processor, document, draft copy, top copy, reference, cursor, keyboard, display screen, hard copy.

2 Type the following text on your word processor, reading it carefully as you do so:

> To use the personal stereo set, you must put in the batteries, plug in the headphones and insert a cassette tape. To put in the batteries, open the lid of the battery compartment and slide the bateries in. Line up the + signs on the batteries with the + signs on the sides of the compartment. Put the headphone plug in the socket on the top of the player, and press it in firmly. When putting in a cassette, open up the cassette lid, and slide in the cassette with the tape side upwards.

Now space out and line up the text so that the instructions are as clear as possible. Mark important words so that they are printed in bold or italics, or are underlined.

Print the new version of the text. Compare it with the original text above, and comment on the improvements in clarity.

3 Type a brief description of your school career on a word processor. Describe the subjects you are taking, the sports you play, and your hobbies and interests. Set out the information as clearly as possible. Use headings and underlined and bold text where appropriate.

4 Devise a simple system of names for the references to documents stored on a disk. Use a suitable code for the type of document, the subject and the date. Look at the example in Section 2.1.

5 Type a short paragraph in French or German on your word processor. Then translate it into English, using the space below the paragraph to type the English words and phrases, and then the complete sentences. Here are some passages in French which you might like to try:

a) Mon voisin Charles a un petit chat. Ce chat s'appelle Edouard. Il est tout noir avec une tache blanche sur le museau.

b) Emily et Alfred vont faire des courses aujourd'hui. Ils veulent acheter des vêtements: une robe, un pantalon, des chaussettes et un cadeau pour leur maman. Ils se trouvent à l'arrêt de bus et attendent l'autobus.

c) L'hiver passé, nous sommes allés skier en Suisse. Notre professeur de ski, Anna, nous a appris comment tenir debout sur nos skis et comment s'arrêter. C'est la première fois que je skiais mais cela m'a beaucoup plu. Je suis tombée plusieurs fois mais sans jamais me faire mal.

Repeat this process, starting with suitable paragraphs in English and translating to another language.

31

6 Decide on the outline of a short story. Type this outline on a word processor, and print a copy of it for each member of a group of pupils. Then assign each member of the group a part of the story to write.

Each member of the group enters his or her part of the story as a separate document. Then read these documents, as blocks of text, into a single document which contains the whole story. Edit the story to correct any errors and print it.

7 Use a word processor for any of the following:

a) typing essays or poems, in English or another language;

b) producing a report of an experiment you have done in a science class;

c) producing a fieldwork report for geography or environmental science;

d) if you can pick up French or German television, produce a news summary in French or German after watching the television news in that language.

Things to Find Out

1 Find out whether companies in your area are using word processors. Find out what tasks are done on them, and what benefits they have brought.

2 Find out the cost of a simple word processor, or a computer which can be used for word processing. Also find out the cost of an electric typewriter. Comment on the difference in cost.

3 Find out what job opportunities there are in your area for people who can use word processors. Find out what the salaries are for these jobs, and comment on them.

4 Find out how many of the pupils in your class, form or year group have word processors at home. Comment on your findings.

Points to Discuss

1 Read the two stories at the start of this chapter. Discuss the advantages and disadvantages of word processing, as they appear in the stories. Also discuss the differences in the types of work done by the people in the stories. Would you prefer to work with a typewriter, or with a word processor?

2 Word processors enable fewer people to do more work than could be done with typewriters. In some companies this has led to losses of jobs. Discuss this situation.

3 Word processors make it possible for some people to work at home. They enable disabled people, and mothers of small children to have jobs based at home. Discuss these effects of word processing.

4 When newspapers changed to the use of word processors, many printers and other workers lost their jobs. Find out what happened during these changes, and comment on them.

CHAPTER 3

Information storage and retrieval

● Peter Brown, the sales manager of a company which makes jeans, is planning a sales trip. He wants to visit all the shops in a certain area which have bought jeans from his company recently, to show them the new range. He asks Carol Grimes, his secretary, to make a list of all the shops he will visit.

Carol uses the card index with the names of all the company's customers. She works her way through the cards, writing down the name and address of each shop in the required area,

which has recently bought jeans from the company. After a while, she realises that her list is getting very long, and many of the shops have only

bought small numbers of jeans. She tells Peter, who decides to visit only those shops which have bought more than a certain number recently.

Carol starts again, crossing off all the shops whose orders were too low. She continues to the end of the card index, and then types the list. She has to work late to finish it.

● Anita Jackson, sales manager of a nearby company which makes T-shirts, is also planning a sales trip. She would like to visit all the shops in a certain area which buy T-shirts from her company, to show them the new range. She asks her assistant, Brian Jones, to produce a list of the shops.

Brian uses his desktop computer to call up a file of all the company's customers. He selects from the file all the shops in the required area which have bought T-shirts recently. The list is displayed on the screen, and Brian realises that it is too long for

Anita to visit in the available time. He tells Anita. She decides to visit only the shops which have bought more than a certain number recently. Brian selects these shops, prints the list of their names and addresses, and takes the list to Anita. It has taken him ten minutes.

```
RECORD # 00001
CLIENT      :Short Sharp Shirts  :
CONTACT     :David Sharp         :
ADDRESS1    :23 High Street      :
ADDRESS2    :Kingston            :
ADDRESS3    :Surrey             ■:
POSTCODE    :KT10 6VT  :
TELNO       :01 337 5983 :
AREACODE    :SE17:
SALES       :    945.37:
```

QUESTIONS

1 How long did Carol Grimes take to produce a list of the required shops?
How long did Brian Jones take?
Comment on your answers.

2 When Peter and Anita changed their minds about the shops they were going to visit, how much more work did it cause for Carol and Brian?
Comment on your answers.

3 a) What information was used to produce the lists in each story?
b) What **two** conditions were used to select the final list of shops in each story?

4 What other advantages does a computer system have over a card index for storing information about customers and sales?

3.1 Information Storage and Retrieval

The computer in the second story above is used to store information and then retrieve it. The information is stored in files.

- **Files**: In the story, there is a file with information about all the company's customers. The file consists of a number of *records*.

- **Records**: In the story, there is one record for each customer. Figure 3.1 shows a typical record. Each record consists of a number of *fields*.

- **Fields**: There is a field for the name of the company, one for each line of the address, and so on. Some of the fields contain codes, such as the area code.

```
CLIENT:   SIR T SHIRTS

ADDRESS:  30 HIGH STREET
          WESTHAMPTON
          SURREY

POSTCODE: TW8 4MT          AREA CODE:  SUR B7

TEL CODE: 0933             TEL NO:  78556

PURCHASE TOTALS:

JAN 86:  £395.00           FEB 86:  £420.00

MAR 86:  £987.00           APR 86:  £865.00
```

Figure 3.1: Printout of record in company cutomer sales file

Files, records and fields are the most convenient way of arranging information so that it can be stored and retrieved by computer. Deciding what information to include in a file, and how to set it out, is a very important part of information management.

Information retrieval systems, or **database systems**, can be used for a number of tasks. (Database systems can do much more than store and retrieve information, but the differences are not important for this course.) They allow you to carry out the following tasks:

- Create files, and enter records. Records can be edited, new records can be inserted and unwanted records can be deleted.

- View records on the computer screen.

- Select records under certain conditions, for example all the customers in a certain area.

- Print fields from selected records, such as the name and address of selected customers.

Information retrieval systems can also calculate totals of the numbers in certain fields, and process the information in other ways. Some of them can produce tables which can be copied into word processor documents.

● **A C T I V I T Y**

3.2 **School Club Members**

In this section, you will use an information retrieval system to create a file of the members of a school club. You will enter records for the members, and select records under certain conditions.

Either choose an existing school club, such as the stamp club, **or** invent a new club for this activity. (How about a fan club for your favourite pop star or local football club?) If you choose an existing club, get permission from the membership secretary to use the list of members.

First of all, decide what fields to include in each record. The photograph shows one way of setting out the records, but it is not the only way. For example, the member's name can be one field or two — one for the first name and one for the surname. Make sure that there are enough fields for long addresses. Decide which fields can be in code, and work out suitable codes. Think carefully about how you are going to use the records. This will help you to decide what fields to include.

When you have decided what fields to include, write down a list of the names of the fields, and the number of characters in each. It should look something like this:

Firstname:	10	characters
Surname:	10	characters
Boy/Girl:	1	character
Form:	3	characters
Address 1:	20	characters
Address 2:	20	characters
Address 3:	20	characters
Postcode:	8	characters
Telno:	8	characters
Years:	1	character

Note that the last field — the number of years that a person has been a member — is a number which may be used to select groups of members. For example, you might want a list of all those who have been members for more than two years. In some information retrieval systems, fields which are numbers must be identified as such.

Three of the fields contain **codes**. These are the form and postcode fields, and the field for boy or girl. Boys have the code B and girls have the code G. Codes are short ways of representing information. They save space and make it easy to select groups of records.

Run the information retrieval program on your school's computer. Look at the instructions for the program to find out how to carry out each operation.

- Create a new file, with records set out as you have planned. If necessary, distinguish between fields which contain numbers and those which contain characters.

- Enter the information for some or all of the members, and save it on disk. (This will take some time!)

- Look at the records on the computer screen, and check them carefully. Correct any mistakes you find.

- Print the records.

- Save the records on disk, if the program does not do this automatically. Before you leave the information retrieval program, make sure that the information has been saved on disk!

When the records for all the members have been entered and checked, they can be used for a number of purposes. One is described in the next activity, others are given in the exercise at the end of this chapter.

QUESTIONS

1 Why is it important to plan the fields in a record very carefully?

2 Why are codes useful for some items of information?

3 Compare the fields you have chosen with those selected for other clubs. Comment on the differences.

● **ACTIVITY**

3.3 **Address Labels**

In this section you will use the file of club members to print a set of address labels for a selected group.

First decide on the group for whom the labels will be produced. It may be all the girls (or all the boys), or all those who have been a member for a certain period of time. It may be all those who live in a certain area — letters in the postcode can be used to identify areas.

Then decide what information you want for the address labels, and how it is to be set out (see Figure 3.2).

- Run the information retrieval program on your school's computer, and call up the club membership file.

Figure 3.2

```
SALLY BOWLES
23 ASH GROVE
FORMBY
LANCASHIRE      L23 9BJ
```

- Enter the condition to select the records you want. These will be copied to another file. Enter the name of the new file.

- Call up the file containing the selected records, and enter the names of the fields to be printed. Set out the information in the layout you require.

- Print the address labels. If you are using adhesive labels, be careful not to jam the printer!

QUESTIONS

1 How long did it take you to print the address labels on the computer?
How long would it have taken you to copy out or type the labels?
Comment on your answers.

2 How useful are codes when selecting groups of records?

ACTIVITY 3.4 **Wildlife Survey**

In this section, a group of pupils will carry out a survey of the wildlife — birds, animals, plants — found near the school. The records of the observations will be entered on an information retrieval system. The aim is to find out what types of wildlife there are, how many of each type are seen, where they are to be found, and what they are doing. This activity can form the basis of a class project which extends over a period of time.

First decide what types of wildlife you will observe, and list some of the ways in which the results will be used. For example, you may wish to study birds in a nearby wood, and try to find out which types of birds live in which parts of the wood. You may want to calculate the total number of each type of bird observed in each area.

Get some pictures of the birds, animals, insects, fish or plants that you are going to look for, and make sure that you can all identify them!

It is a good idea to draw a sketch map of the area to be surveyed, and divide the area into blocks. Give each block a code for easy identification. If possible, plan the blocks so that one entire block can be observed at one time.

Now plan how the observations are going to be recorded. You may decide to observe for a fixed period of time (say a quarter of an hour) and make one record for each type of bird, animal, fish or insect observed during that time. Design a record card to be filled in while you are observing, and the fields of the computer record to be entered later. Think carefully about the information you want to be recorded, and plan suitable codes for fields as necessary. Figure 3.3 shows an example of a record card.

- Either draw up a number of record cards, or produce them on the word processing program on your computer.
- Assign blocks on the map to members of the group.
- Go out to the areas and fill in one record card for each species you observe during the allocated time.

Wildlife Survey

Species:_____

Date:_____ Area:_____

Time Started:_____ Time ended:_____

Number seen:_____

Activities Observed:_____

_____

_____

_____

_____

_____

Observed By:_____

Figure 3.3: Wildlife survey card

Be careful not to damage any plants or injure any birds or animals while you are doing the survey.

- Get one member of the group to create a file on the school's computer for the wildlife survey records.
- Take turns to enter your records into the file. Check the information very carefully, and correct any mistakes. Save all the information on disk.

The observations may be repeated a number of times, in order to build up a good supply of information. When sufficient records have been entered, they can be studied in a number of ways. Some suggestions are as follows:

- each member of the group chooses one species to follow up;
- the member selects all the records of observations of his or her chosen species, and copies them to a separate file;
- look at the file, and plot the observations on the sketch map of the area. Use the computer to add up the total of the numbers observed;
- write a report on the observed activities of the chosen species. Produce the reports on a word processor if possible.

```
RECORD # 00001
SPECIES    :Swan
OBSERVER   :Susan Hollingsworth :
DATE       :22nd Oct 1986      :
STARTTIME  :11:45:
ENDTIME    :12:00:
PLACECODE  :DF08:
NOSEEN     :    3:
NOTES1     :Two adult swans, one baby:
NOTES2     :Swimming together
NOTES3     :Eating bread thrown into :
NOTES4     :the river by people      :
NOTES5     :■
```

QUESTIONS

1 What are the benefits of using a computer to store and retrieve the observations?

2 Did you change the structure of the records during the survey? If so, why? If not, would you have liked to add more fields? Comment on your answers.

3.5 Computer Elements: Disks

Magnetic disks are used to store large quantities of information. A computer can read information from a disk and write it to a disk very quickly. The information remains on the disk even when the computer is switched off.

Microcomputers use small single disks, as shown in the photograph. They are made of plastic, and coated with a substance which can be magentised. Large computers use **disk packs**, which contain a number of metal disks on a single shaft. Disks are placed in **disk drives**, which spin them round very fast, and allow information to be **read** from them and written to them.

The disk drives on an ICL mainframe computer. There is a disk pack on top of the right-hand drive.

Most disks can be removed from the drives and stored when not in use. Disks can usually be swapped between computers of the same type. Some computers have **Winchester disks** which can store very large amounts of information, but which cannot be removed from their drive.

QUESTIONS

1 What two substances are used to make magnetic disks?

2 What are the advantages of being able to exchange disks between two computers?

3 What is the advantage of Winchester disks over other types of disk? What is their disadvantage?

3.6 Information Retrieval in Practice

Information retrieval systems and databases are widely used in industry and commerce. Their introduction has meant that card indexes are now much less common. Computers are used to store information about customers and sales, as described at the beginning of this chapter. They are also used to keep records of the work done by gas and electricity maintenance engineers. Mail order companies use databases to keep records of their sales, and their stocks of goods. Some doctors use information retrieval systems for their patient records — see Section 3.7.

Many clubs and societies keep their membership records on computers, and some schools use similar systems for their pupil records. Some churches keep their parish records on computer. Many companies keep their staff records on similar systems. Social Security records are gradually being transferred to a very large computer system. A great deal of research at universities is done using database systems to store the results.

The police in Britain have a number of large files on the **Police National Computer**. One contains a list of all the cars which have been reported stolen anywhere in Britain. Another contains details of all the cars in Britain — their registration mark, description and name and address of their owner. A third file has information about all the people who are wanted by the police, or have been reported missing. There is also a list of all the people who have criminal records.

A terminal at a police station, which can be linked to the Police National Computer. It includes a small telephone switchboard and a radio link.

The files on the Police National Computer can be examined from terminals at every police station in Britain. Police officers can contact the stations by radio, and have information from the computer files reported to them by the duty officer.

Police forces are beginning to use computers for the investigation of serious crimes. These store all the information which is received about the crime, and build up indexes to the information. They enable large amounts of information to be scanned very quickly. They save time, and help to ensure that important information is not lost in a mass of details.

A policeman in radio contact with his station. This gives him instant access to police computers for information.

QUESTIONS

1 List some uses of information retrieval systems:
   a) in business;   b) in education;   c) in government.
   Include in your list ones mentioned in the text and others you have found out yourself.

2 a) List **four** types of information stored on police computers.
   b) Suggest some uses for this information.
   c) Discuss the problems which could be caused:
      (i) if information on the police computers is wrong;
      (ii) if the information got into the wrong hands.
   d) Suggest some further uses of computers for police work.
   Discuss the benefits and possible problems of each.

3 Design suitable records for each of the four files on the Police National Computer. Choose suitable codes for any fields which require them.

3.7 Privacy of Personal Information

• Dr David Evans and his colleague, Dr Susan Metcalfe, at present store all the records about their patients on card files. They are in large filing cabinets, and are rather awkward to use. Patients with serious illnesses have records which contain hundreds of sheets of paper.

Dr Evans and Dr Metcalfe are discussing the use of a computer for their records. Each patient would have a set of records in the file. These would contain notes on the symptoms the patient had, such as a headache. They would also have the doctor's diagnosis of the illness. Most important, they would contain lists of the medicines which have been prescribed for the patient. The computer would make things much easier in the surgery!

But there is a problem. All the information on the files is personal. Doctors are not allowed to reveal the contents of a patient's medical record to anyone - not even the patient. However, if the records are placed on a computer, they will be covered by the **Data Protection Act**. This regulates the storage of personal information by computer. It also permits people to see their own records, and to insist that they are corrected if they contain errors.

The conversation between the two doctors goes like this:

Dr Evans: Putting our medical records on a computer will make things much easier. We shall be able to find the information we want much more quickly. We can keep a much better check on the medicines we prescribe.

Dr Metcalfe: But if we do that, the patients will be able to see their own records. They won't understand most of what is on them, because it is in medical language.

Dr Evans: We can always explain things they don't understand. Knowing more about what is wrong with them might help. It might make some of them better at taking the medicines we prescribe!

Dr Metcalfe: I suspect that some of my patients have cancer. I have noted this on their records, but I don't want to tell them until I am more certain. What if they saw their records?

Dr Evans: As long as they know that it is only a possibility, it shouldn't worry them too much. The computer will help us to look for patterns in these cases. We might be able to help people before serious symptoms appear.

QUESTIONS

1 Working in pairs, continue this discussion between the two doctors. Think of further benefits of putting medical records on computer, and of further problems which could arise.

2 a) List the uses of medical records mentioned in the above passage.
b) Suggest or find out further uses for medical records kept on a computer. These may be at doctor's surgeries and at hospitals.

3 Draw up a set of suitable fields for a medical record. One record is filled in each time a patient visits the doctor.

Exercise 3

1 Write down the meanings of the following words or phrases: card index, file, record, field, information retrieval system, database system, disk, disk pack, disk drive, Winchester disk.

The next few questions contain suggestions for further activites using the information retrieval system on your school computer.

2 Design a record to store all the information needed about a book in the school library. Use the library card index system to help you in the design. Think carefully about the way in which this information is used, or could be used. Discuss the uses of a computerised records system with the school librarian.

Decide on suitable fields for the record, and choose codes for those fields which need them. Make sure that fields are large enough for long names!

Create a file for library book records using the fields you have designed. Enter the information for a selection of books. Use the information retrieval system to select books under various conditions. Try conditions such as all the Fiction books, or all those bought in 1984. Comment on the advantages of your system.

Make a list of all the ways in which a library book records system could be used, if there was a computer in the school library.

3 Design a record for a file for you to use as a personal address book. Allocate fields for the name, address and telephone number of each person, and perhaps a secret code for how much you like them!

Enter the names of some or all of your friends into the file. Use the computer to look up addresses and telephone numbers.

4 Plan a survey of local amenities, to be carried out by a group of pupils. Obtain or sketch a map of the area to be surveyed, and draw up a list of the types of amenities to be investigated. Then design a report form to be filled in by the pupils carrying out the survey, and the fields of a record for each amenity to be entered on the computer. Some suggestions are given below.

Types of amenity —

Community: Libraries, youth clubs, clinics, old people's centres, etc.

Sport and Leisure: Swimming baths, sports clubs, dance centres, etc.

Entertainment: Theatres, cinemas, discos, etc.

Information on each amenity:

Name, address and telephone number
Hours of opening
Facilities provided
Cost
Restrictions on entry (e.g. no-one under 18)

Carry out the survey, and enter the results into the file. Select groups of amenities by type, area and opening times, and mark the amenities on the map of the area.

5 Plan a survey, to be carried out by a group of pupils, of sites in your area of historical importance. Use the steps from Question 4 to help with the survey.

6 Experiment with some additional uses of the club membership file from the first activity in this chapter.

a) Print an attendance register for club meetings.
b) If the club charges fees, use the file to keep records of when fees are due, and when they are paid.
c) If the club organises outings, mark member's records when they have paid to go on an outing, and then print a list of those going.

7 Write a detective story in which the police computer plays an important part. Make the story as realistic as possible, and do not exaggerate the way in which the computer can be used.

Things to Find Out

1 Find out whether any companies in your area use information retrieval systems or databases. If so, find out for what purposes they are used, and what benefits they have brought.

2 If your school has a computerised system for pupil records, find out how it is used. (You will not be allowed to see the records on it, as most of the information is confidential.) Find out what advantages it has over the previous system (usually records kept on cards).

3 Find out whether any of the doctor's surgeries near your school use computers for their medical records. Also find out if any local hospitals keep their patient records on computer. If so, find out what are the benefits of the new system, and whether there have been any problems.

4 Postcodes are very useful ways of grouping people by the area in which they live. The letters and numbers in the code are used to identify areas — a complete postcode identifies a short row of houses or one large building.

Find out how the postcode system in Britain works. Discuss ways in which postcodes can be used in records kept by businesses.

5 The **Royal Society for the Protection of Birds (RSPB)** uses computers for its membership records. It also has an information retrieval system containing records of rare birds.
a) Find out more about how computers are used by the RSPB.
b) Find out whether your wildlife survey provides any information which is useful to the RSPB.

Points to Discuss

1 Many of the information retrieval systems discussed in this chapter are used to store personal information - people's names, addresses, telephone numbers, and information about illnesses they have had or crimes they have committed.

Personal information of this sort, stored on a computer, may not be disclosed to anyone who wants to see it. There is a law in the United Kingdom — the **Data Protection Act** — which controls the way personal information on computers is used.

When a file of personal information is set up, the organisation which has set up the file must apply to the **Data Protection Registrar** to register the file. The application includes a list of the uses of the information, and a list of the people or organisations who will be able to see it. The people who are listed in the file must give permission for the information about them to be used in the ways proposed. They have the right to inspect their own records and to request that any errors in them are corrected.

Imagine that you had to apply for registration of the club membership file set up in the first activity in this chapter.
a) Draw up a list of the people or organisations which would be allowed to see the club membership records.
b) Draw up a list of all the ways in which the information is to be used.
c) Draw up a list of the precautions you would take against people stealing the information.
d) Use a word processor to produce a note to all the members, asking their permission to use the information in the ways proposed.
e) Discuss the issue of privacy of information from the point of view of the members of the club.

2 Some uses of computers are exempt from the Data Protection Act. Find out what they are. Discuss the reasons for their exemption.

3 The Data Protection Act allows people to see copies of their own records, if they are stored on computers. They can object if there are any mistakes in the information stored about them. Discuss the consequences of this.

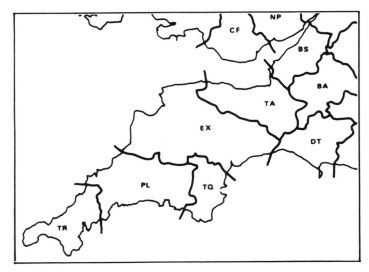

Spreadsheets

● David Edwards, the sales manager of a company which sells hi-fi sets, is preparing his **sales forecast** for the new year. The forecast is an estimate of how many of each type of hi-fi set the company will sell in the coming year.

David takes the printout from the company's computer which shows the results for the previous year. He draws up a table, with columns for the products, and rows for the months of the year. Each item in the table is the sum of money earned from the sales of one type of hi-fi in one month.

David works through the previous year's figures. He estimates by how much each figure will change from last year to this year. He uses his calculator to work out the new figures, and writes the answers down in the table. When he has finished, he adds up the rows, to see how much will be earned each month. The column totals show how much will be earned by each product.

Some of the totals look too high. David makes another estimate of the way some of the sales will change, and changes the figures. He re-calculates the totals which are affected. When he is satisfied, he gives the table to his secretary to type. She notices a mistake in one of his figures, and brings the table back to him. David corrects the figure, and once again adds up the totals which are affected. His secretary finishes typing the table.

Later David presents his forecast at a meeting of the managers of the company. They do not agree with some of the figures, and David is asked to change them. He alters them, and once again calculates the totals. He gives the new table to his secretary to type. Once again, she notices a mistake in the calculations...

BEST BUY HI-FI P.L.C.
Sales Forecasts (£ thousands) Model Month

Month	'Cruiseman' cassette player	'Echo Blaster'	'Music Maker' midi	'Lasersound' CD player	'Sound City' music system	Monthly total (all models)
Jan	612	247	479	46 ~~50~~	187	1578
Feb	463	202	451	47	174	1337
Mar	419	187	432	45	161	1244
Apr	376	162	401	45	149	1133
May	398	159	363	41	133	1094
Jun	404 ~~454~~	151	321	39	119	34 ~~1087~~
Jul	407	155	350	35	105 ~~97~~	1048
Aug	422	165	370	29	112	91 ~~1083~~
Sep	487	175	401	28	127	1201
Oct	594	189	423	34	152	1367
Nov	708	229	477	41	176	1607
Dec	789	269	491 ~~545~~	48	96	1773 ~~1828~~
Annual total per model	6079 ~~6129~~	2288	4959 ~~5017~~	478 ~~482~~	1688	500 ~~15608~~

45

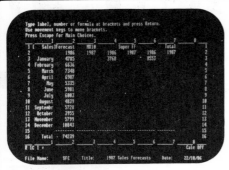

● A year later, Spencer Jackson, the new sales manager of the company, is preparing the sales forecast. He uses his desktop computer to set up a **spreadsheet**, a table of rows and columns of figures. He sets up a column for each product, and a row for each month of the year. In the space for each number he places a formula to calculate the new year's sales figures form those of the previous year. He sets up a column for the total sales for each month. He also sets up a row for the total sales of each product.

He enters the previous year's figures from the computer printout of the sales. He enters some percentage changes for the sales, and watches while the computer calculates all the new sales figures, and the totals. One of the figures is obviously wrong. Spencer checks the formula for the number and corrects it. The spreadsheet automatically calculates all the numbers and totals again.

Some of the totals look too optimistic. Spencer changes some of the percentages. The spreadsheet program re-calculates the sales, and adds up all the totals again. When he is satisfied, Spencer prints a number of copies of the table, and sends them to his colleagues.

A few days later, Spencer discusses the figures with the other managers of the company. There is a desktop computer at the meeting, and they look at the spreadsheet on the screen. The other managers do not agree with some of the forecasts, so Spencer changes the percentages, and re-calculates the figures. When they are agreed on the forecasts, Spencer prints a copy of the table for each of them.

QUESTIONS

1 How did David Edwards calculate the sales figures? How did Spencer Jackson calculate the sales figures?

2 How were errors corrected in each case? Comment on your answers.

3 What did David Edwards do when one of the sales figures needed to be changed? What did Spencer Jackson do?

   Comment on your answers.

4 a) Estimate how long it took to produce each sales forecast. Comment on your answers.
   b) List all the benefits in using a spreadsheet for sales forecasts. Include those implied in the stories, and any others you can think of.

4.1 A Spreadsheet Program

A spreadsheet program allows you to create tables of numbers, set out in rows and columns. Each item in the table is a **cell**. A cell can contain a number, or a formula which calculates the number in the cell. Alternatively, a cell can contain a label, such as the heading of a column.

Formulae can be used for any type of calculation, including row or column totals. Formulae usually refer to cells by their row and column numbers. For example, the formula

$$R4C7 = R4C6 - R4C5$$

uses the number in Row 4, Column 6 and subtracts the number in Row 4, Column 5. The result goes into Row 4, Column 7.

Some spreadsheet programs use letters for columns and numbers for rows. For example, the cell B7 is the seventh row of the second column. The above formula becomes

$$G4 = F4 - E4$$

Spreadsheets can be saved on disk, and read back from disk when they are needed again. They can be printed. Some spreadsheet programs allow spreadsheets to be transferred to other programs, such as word processors or information retrieval programs. Others have facilities to plot graphs of the numbers in a spreadsheet.

A spreadsheet showing the weekly attendance figures of a class.

QUESTIONS

1 How are numbers in a spreadsheet set out?

2 What **three** types of information can be contained in one cell in a spreadsheet?

3 Explain in words what the following spreadsheet formula means:

$$R4C6 = R2C6 - R3C6$$
$$(\text{or } F4 = D4 - E4)$$

4 In what way can spreadsheet programs be linked to word processing programs?

● **ACTIVITY**

4.2 Invoices

An **invoice** is produced whenever goods are bought by one company from another. It shows the quantities and prices of each item, the amounts (quantity times price) and the total amount. There is also an invoice number and a date.

In this section, you will use a spreadsheet program on your school's computer to produce an invoice like the one on the next page.

Run the spreadsheet program on your school's computer. Look at the instructions for the program to see how to carry out each operation.

```
Invoice         Date:
Quantity   Item   Price   Amount


                   Total:   _____
                            _____
```

- Create a new spreadsheet, and type the labels for the invoice as shown.

- Set the numbers in the quantity column to be whole numbers (integers), and those in the price and amounts column to be currency.

- Type the formulae for the amounts. If your spreadsheet uses numbers for rows and columns, then the formula for the first amount, in Row 6 Column 4, is

$$R6C4 = R6C1 * R6C3$$

If it uses letters for the columns and numbers for the rows, the formula is

$$D6 = A6 * C6$$

Note that * is used for multiplication, and / for division in most spreadsheets.

Think carefully about the formulae for the other amounts, and type them in. Then type the formula for the total. If you have left three rows for items, then it is in Row 10 Column 4. It is the sum of the numbers from Row 6 Column 4 to Row 8 Column 4:

$$R10C4 = sum(R6C4:R8C4)$$
$$or\ D10 = sum(D6:D8)$$

- Check the spreadsheet very carefully, and correct any errors. Then save the blank invoice on disk.

- Now call up the blank invoice, and type some entries into it. The invoice in the margin shows some examples.

```
Invoice:   A0001   Date:   27/05/86
Quantity   Item    Price   Amount
      1    Ladder  27.95
     12    Paint    7.45
      4    Brush    3.25

                    Total:  _____
                            _____
```

- Switch calculation on, if it is not already on. The amounts and the total amount are calculated and displayed.

- Print the invoice.

- Now read the blank invoice from disk, and fill in another set of figures. Use a different invoice number. Switch calculation on, and then print the invoice.

- Again call up the blank invoice from disk. Add two cells, one for the VAT, and one for the price plus VAT. Work out the formulae for yourself. (VAT is 15% of the total amount.)

- Save the modified invoice on disk. Enter some figures into it, and calculate the amounts, total amount, VAT and total plus VAT. Print the invoice.

QUESTIONS

1 When are invoices produced in practice?

2 Why is the blank invoice saved on disk, before it is filled in?

4.3 **Football League Table**

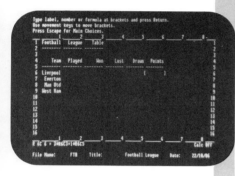

The spreadsheet in the margin is set out as a football league table. It shows the number of matches played, won, lost and drawn, and the points for a number of teams.

- Run the spreadsheet program on your school's computer, and open up a blank spreadsheet.

- Type the headings shown in the spreadsheet.

- Enter the formulae for the points. At present, three points are given for a win, and one for a draw. The first formula in the points column is:

$$R3C6 = 3 * R3C3 + R3C5$$
$$(\text{or } F3 = 3 * C3 + E5)$$

Enter formulae for each team you wish to include. Work out how they change from one row to the next.

- Save the blank spreadsheet on disk.

- Type the names of some football teams into the spreadsheet, and the numbers of games they have played, won, lost and drawn.

- Switch calculation on, and see that the points are calculated.

- Print the spreadsheet.

- Change the formulae to see the effects of changing the way points are allocated. For example, try five points for a win and two for a draw. Also try subtracting points for lost matches.

- When you have changed all the formulae for a new system of points, print the league table again.

QUESTIONS

1 Why is the blank table saved on disk, before the information for the teams is filled in?

2 Do the differences in the methods of awarding points make any difference in the order of the teams in the league?

● **ACTIVITY**

4.4 Hire Purchase Calculations

Many shops sell goods by **hire purchase**. Instead of paying the full amount for the item, payment is spread over a period of time. A **deposit** is paid when the item is bought. Regular **payments** are made, usually once a month, until the item has been paid for. The total amount paid by hire purchase is more than the cash price of the item.

A spreadsheet can easily be used to set out hire purchase calculations.

- Run the spreadsheet program on your school's computer, and open up a blank spreadsheet.

- Type the headings shown in the photograph.

- Set the second, fourth, fifth and sixth columns to show numbers as currency.

- The total hire purchase price is the deposit plus the number of payments times the amount of each payment. In the spreadsheet above, the formula for the first total is

$$R3C5 = R3C2 + R3C3 * R3C4$$
$$(or\ E3 = B3 + C3 * D3)$$

Type this formula into cell R3C5 (E3).

- Work out the formulae for the totals in the next few rows and type them in.

- Save the spreadsheet on disk.

- Now enter the details for a number of items. Either visit a local shop and write them down, or make them up. Enter the name, deposit, number of payments and amount of each payment. Also enter the cash price in its column.

- Switch calculation on, and see that the total hire purchase prices are calculated.

- Print the spreadsheet.

- Enter a new column for the difference between the hire purchase price and the cash price. Work out the formulae you need, and type them in. Calculate the differences, and print the spreadsheet.

QUESTIONS

1 What are the benefits of hire purchase payments?

2 What is the disadvantage of hire purchase payments?

3 Did you save any time by doing the hire purchase calculations on a spreadsheet? Comment on your answer.

4.5 Computer Elements: Memory and Silicon Disks

The ROM cartridge used by a BBC Master series microcomputer.

A high-capacity memory chip.

The **memory** of a computer stores the information and instructions which the computer is using at the time. For example, the spreadsheet which a computer is working on is stored in memory. Information can be transferred to or from memory very quickly.

A computer memory consists of a number of **chips**. Each memory chip can hold tens or hundreds of thousands of items of information or program instructions. It contains a large number of identical electrical circuits, as shown in the photograph. Memory chips are mounted in **printed circuit boards** inside the computer.

There are two type of memory chips. **ROM** chips keep a permanent copy of their contents, even when the computer is switched off. They store programs which are used frequently. Some ROM chips are in cartridges which can be plugged into the computer when they are needed. **RAM** chips hold information which can be changed by the computer at any time. When the computer is switched off, the contents of the RAM chips is lost.

On some computers it is possible to use a portion of RAM as if it were backing store. This creates a **silicon disk**, which can transfer files to and from memory much more quickly than ordinary magnetic disks. The only problem is that files on silicon disk are lost when the computer is switched off!

A silicon disk is ideal as a temporary store for files while they are being used intensively. It is particularly useful when the computer is attached to a network. Transferring files to and from the central network disks is a slow process. If a silicon disk is available, the files which are needed are loaded onto it at the start of the session. All reading and writing of files during the session is very quick, as the files are on silicon disk. At the end of the session, the files are copied back to the network disk.

QUESTIONS

1 How are memory chips mounted inside a computer?

2 What are the two types of memory chips?

3 Why are ROM chips very useful?

4 What are the advantages and disadvantages of silicon disks?

5 Why are silicon disks particularly useful on a network of computers?

4.6 Spreadsheets in Practice

Spreadsheets are a relatively new use of computers. Their main use is in business, for planning purposes. The story at the start of this chapter explains how they are used in this way. Their main benefit is that the plans can easily be changed, and all the numbers in the spreadsheet can be re-calculated automatically. They save hours of work with a calculator, and enable plans to be made much more carefully.

Spreadsheets are used by small businesses to produce invoices, as described in the first activity in this chapter. They may be used to keep accounts, and for stock control. They can also be used to plan projects like the construction of large buildings.

Spreadsheets can be used for a variety of mathematical problems. They allow you to investigate number patterns, and set out difficult calculations. Many people with home computers use them to keep accounts, and to plan how they are going to spend their money.

A large construction site — computers are used to manage all the information for a project of this nature.

QUESTIONS

1 What is the main use of spreadsheets?

2 How can spreadsheets be used on home computers?

3 a) In what **four** ways can spreadsheets be used in business?
   b) Suggest some additional uses for spreadsheets in business.

4.7 Computers and Unemployment

• Peter Barnes worked for the same company for twenty-five years. His job was to work out the quantities of materials required for construction projects. It was quite a difficult job, needing knowledge he had built up over the years.

He studied the information about each project, and used it to estimate what materials would be needed. He then looked up the prices of the materials in tables. He filled in a large form, listing the quantities and prices, and used his calculator to work out the costs. He then got one of his colleagues to check all the figures. A large project needed many forms, and took several weeks to complete.

One Monday morning, when he arrived for work, he was called to see his manager. His manager told him that he was being made redundant. The company was introducing computers to calculate the materials needed for projects. The work would be able to be done by half the number of staff that were needed previously. Because of Peter's age, it was not worth re-training him to use the computers.

Peter was given three month's pay. He spent the rest of the day clearing his desk, and then left for the last time.

QUESTIONS

1 Why was Peter not re-trained to use computers in his work?

2 What are the chances of Peter finding a similar job at another company?

3 Think carefully about the situation Peter Barnes found himself in. Suggest some things that could be done by:
a) his company;
b) the local authority;
c) the government;
d) Peter Barnes himself.

Exercise 4

1 Write down the meanings of the following terms: printout, spreadsheet, cell, invoice, hire purchase, memory, chip, printed circuit board, ROM, RAM, silicon disk.

2 Find out what rates of interest are available on money saved with banks, building societies and the post office. Set up a spreadsheet to see the effects of these rates, as follows:

	Rate (%)	Amount	1 Year	2 Years	3 Years	4 Years
Halifax						
Woolwich						
Abbey Nt						
Natnwide						

Set Column 2 to show numbers to one decimal place. Set the columns from 3 onwards to show currency. Include columns for more than four years if you wish.

Column 3 is for the amount invested. Column 4 is for the amount after one year, after interest has been added.

Enter the names of the banks and building societies into the first column, and the interest rates into the second column.

The interest added each year is the rate times the amount, divided by 100. This is added to the amount at the end of the year. The formula for the money after one year in the first row is:

$$R3C4 = R3C2 * R3C3 / 100 + R3C3$$
$$(or \ D3 = B3 * C3 / 100 + C3)$$

The same process is repeated after the second year, starting with the amount after the first year:

$$R3C5 = R3C2 * R3C4 / 100 + R3C4$$
$$(or \ E3 = B3 * D3 / 100 + D3)$$

Enter the formulae into the cells for the amounts after each year. Some spreadsheet programs allow you to copy a formula from one cell to another, and then modify it. Use this facility if possible.

At this stage, check the spreadsheet carefully and save it on disk.

Now enter some amounts of money into the third column. Set calculation on, and see the amounts after each year for the money saved at the different places. Print the table.

Call up the blank table from disk, and enter a different set of amounts. Once again print the table. Comment on the results.

The exercises below are suitable for groups of between three and five pupils.

3 Carry out a survey of prices at local shops or supermarkets. Decide on a list of goods (preferably food and household goods), and select three or four similar shops which supply them. Make sure that the prices you record are for the same quantity of the goods. For example, do not compare the price of 1lb of cheese at one shop with the price of 1kg of cheese at another shop!

The aim of the activity is to work out the total amount that would be spent at the various shops when you buy different quantities of the items.

Set out a spreadsheet like the one shown below to record the prices.

Item	Unit	Quantity	Fine Food Price	Fine Food Amount	AB Store Price	AB Store Amount
Br Bread	Lge loaf					
Coffee	100 g					
Orange	1 litre					
Marge	500 g					
Sausage	500 g					
Total						

Enter the names of the shops and the items, and set the price and amount columns to show currency. Enter the prices for each shop into its price column.

Enter a set of formulae into the amount columns. The amount is the quantity, in Column 3, times the price. For example, the amount spent on the first item at the first shop has the formula:

$$R5C5 = R5C3 * R5C4$$
$$(or \ E5 = C5 * D5)$$

The formula for the same item at the second shop is:

$$R5C7 = R5C3 * R5C6$$
$$(or \ G5 = C5 * F5)$$

Then enter formulae for the total amounts. These will depend on the number of items in your list.

Check the spreadsheet carefully, and then save it on disk.

Now enter a set of quantities for each of the following doing their weekly shop:

a) a single person;
b) a couple;
c) a family with two children;
d) a family with five children and a grandmother;
e) The catering manager of an old people's home with twenty people.

In each case, estimate how much of each item would be needed. Switch calculation on, and see that the amounts and totals are worked out for each shop.

Print the table. Then read back the blank spreadsheet and enter the quantities for the next group.

When you have printed all the results, study them carefully and comment on them.

4 Keep a record of the way you spend your pocket money over a week. Set out a spreadsheet like the one shown below for the figures. Choose your own categories.

The right-hand column shows the totals spent on each item. The bottom row shows the total amounts spent each week.

Item	Mon	Tue	Wed	Thur	Fri	Sat	Total
Travel							
Clothes							
Food							
Records							
Makeup							
Presents							
Savings							
Other							
Total							

Set Columns 2 to 8 to show numbers as currency. Enter the formulae for the totals in Column 8 and Row 11. The formula for the total in Row 3 Column 8 is:

$$R3C8 = sum(R3C2:R3C7)$$
$$(or \ H3 = sum(B3:G3))$$

Save the blank spreadsheet on disk. Then fill in a set of figures, and calculate the row and column totals. Print the spreadsheet.

Call up the blank spreadsheet again and let someone else fill in their figures. Calculate the totals and print the spreadsheet again.

Add up the amounts spent by all the pupils in the group on each item during each week, and enter them in a blank spreadsheet. Once again calculate the totals and print the spreadsheet.

Comment on the total amounts spent on the various items and the variations of these totals throughout the week.

Things to Find Out

1 Find out whether spreadsheets are used for planning within your school. If so, find out how they are used, and whether they save time. If not, suggest some possible uses for spreadsheets in the running of a school.

2 Find out whether any local businesses use spreadsheets in any way. If so, find out what benefits they are bringing.

Points to Discuss

1 Read the two stories at the beginning of this chapter again. In the second story, different plans for the company could be set up and looked at very quickly — even while a meeting was in progress.

Discuss the benefits to a company of being able to investigate alternative plans in this way. Also discuss the advantages that such a company might have over a competitor company which does not make its plans in this manner.

2 Spreadsheets are opening up a number of new opportunities, for home users of computers. For example, families can plan their household budgets on spreadsheets, and make better use of their money. A spreadsheet can be used to compare the prices of alternative holidays, helping a family to choose the best one.
a) Find out whether any members of your class have home computers with spreadsheet programs. If so, find out how they are used.

b) List some further uses of spreadsheets on home computers.
c) Discuss the benefits of using spreadsheets for these purposes.

3 Look once again at the story of Peter Barnes in Section 4.7. Think about the situation which might have arisen if he had not been made redundant. His company would continue to pay him and his colleagues their wages for doing a job which could be done more quickly by computer, at a fraction of the cost. It is quite likely that other construction companies would be changing to the new methods of estimating quantities for projects.

Discuss what might have happened to the company over the next few years if they had not changed to the new methods. The discussion may be arranged as a debate between those who would favour changing to computers, and making the existing staff redundant, and those who would prefer to keep the old methods and staff.

CHAPTER 5

Stock control

Stanley Duffy works in the warehouse at a factory which makes cookers. His job is to issue the parts from which the cookers are made. He has a card index with information about all the items in the warehouse.

Whenever he gets a request for parts, he fills in a slip. This shows the date, time, part number, number to be issued and the name of the person making the request.

Stanley then looks up the part in his index. He checks that he has enough in stock. If so, he writes the date, issue slip number and number issued on the index card. He works out the new number in stock, and writes it down. He then finds the parts on the shelves, and gives them to the person who has asked for them. He puts the issue slip in a file.

If there are not enough parts in stock, he puts the issue slip on a pile, and checks that the part has been ordered. He tells the person who has asked for them when they will be available.

Every afternoon, when it is not too busy, he looks through the index, and writes down the part numbers of all the items which are running low. He sends the list to the orders department, so that the parts can be re-ordered.

When new stock arrives, Stanley checks that it matches the order. He then fills in a receipt slip, and marks the receipt on the index card for the stock. He puts the parts on their shelf. If there is time, he looks for any issue slips for the part on the pile. He telephones the people who are waiting for the part, to tell them that it has arrived.

● Peter Davies works in the warehouse of a factory which produces records and cassette tapes. The warehouse stores the sleeves, labels, and blank cassettes. It also stores the raw materials from which the records are pressed. Stock control is done by computer. The computer also controls the automatic cranes which load and unload the warehouse shelves.

When he gets a request for an item, Peter enters it at the computer keyboard. He fills in a form on the screen. This shows the part number, number of items requested, and the name of the person making the request. The date and time are filled in automatically, and the issue is given a reference number by the computer. A copy of the form is printed.

The computer then checks that the stock is available. If so, it records the issue and subtracts the number issued from the number in stock. The automatic loader is instructed to fetch the items from the shelves.

If the stock is not available, the issue request is written to a file. The expected delivery date of the stock displayed on the screen. Peter tells the person wanting the items when they will be available.

Once a day, Peter instructs the computer to check the stock file, to see which items are running low. The computer prints a list of these in a few minutes. The list is sent to the purchasing department.

When new stock arrives,

Peter checks it against the order, and fills in a form on the computer screen. He enters the part number, and the number received. The computer adds the number received to the number in stock of the item. It instructs the automatic loader to place the items on the shelves in the place allocated for them. It then prints a list of all the people who are waiting for the item.

QUESTIONS

1 What happens when goods are out-of-stock in the first story? What happens in the second story?

Comment on your answers.

2 How are people who are waiting for stock informed that it has arrived –
a) in the first story?
b) in the second story?

Comment on your answers.

3 The computer program in the second story has a way of working out precisely when new stock needs to be ordered. This keeps stock levels low, but ensures that items are very seldom out-of-stock.
a) How are goods re-ordered in the first story?
b) Is the method of re-ordering in the first story likely to keep such careful control of stock levels?
c) What are the consequences of being out-of-stock?
d) What are the consequences of having too much stock?

Comment on your answers.

A bar code being used to check stock at a supermarket.

The warehouse storing finished goods at a large factory.

Item number:	J61008B
Name:	Dress
Style:	Miranda
Colour:	Apricot
Size:	Medium
Supplier:	A&B Fashions
	25 Wapping Way
	London E11 2WR
Min Stock:	20
Re-Order Qty:	100
No in Stock:	37

Stock control systems are used in shops, factories and warehouses. They keep a check on the movements of goods coming in and out. They have **files** with a **record** for each item in stock. The record has **fields** for the name of the item, its stock number, the name and address of its supplier, and the number in stock. There is also the **minimum stock level**, which is the number below which the stock level must not fall. The **re-order quantity** is the number of items which are ordered when supplies drop below the minimum stock level.

Stock **movement** files are also kept. These have one **record** for each movement of stock into or out of the warehouse. Movement records have fields for the date, and sometimes the time. They include the item number and the quantity added or removed. There is also a reference to the invoice for the purchase or the sale of the goods. Some stock control systems check whether an item has fallen below the minimum stock level whenever a movement takes place. Others check the entire stock file in one operation. Some print orders automatically.

QUESTIONS

1 What information does a movement record contain?

2 What two kinds of files are kept by stock control systems? Describe the fields in a typical record in each.

3 How are goods identified in some stock control systems?

4 How often are stock records brought up-to-date?

5.2 | Stationery Cupboard Stock Control

In this activity you will set up a stock control system for the stationery cupboard in your school, or the book cupboard in one of the departments. You can do it **either** using record cards, **or** on the school's computer.

First of all spend some time discussing the best way of allocating stock numbers to the items. This is not as easy as it seems! You may decide to give every item a different number, or you may decide to group similar items.

For example, exercise books may have several types of lines on the pages. One way of allocating stock numbers is to use the last digit to indicate the type of lines:

Item		Stock Number
Exercise Book	Wide Lines	1001
Exercise Book	Narrow Lines	1002
Exercise Book	Squared Pages	1003
Exercise Book	Blank Pages	1004

When you have decided on a numbering scheme, set out the stock records for your system. There is one record for each item. Look at the photograph in the previous section and decide what fields to include. Use codes for fields where they are suitable.

- **Either** draw up a set of record cards, one for each item in stock **or** set up a computer file for the stock records. Use a stock control program if one is available. If not, you may be able to use an information retrieval program (see Chapter 3).

- Design a slip to record the addition or removal of stock. Decide what information to include, and how to set it out. Even if you are using a computer file for stock records, it is useful to have these records on paper.

- Count the number of each item in stock, and write these numbers on the record cards, or enter them into the stock records.

- Now record a series of stock movements. When a set of books is taken from the cupboard:

     Fill in an issue slip;

     Look up the stock record on the file, or on the computer;

     Subtract the number issued from the number in stock.

   In a similar way, fill in a slip when a set of books is put into the cupboard.

- After a number of movements have been recorded, count up the number of each item in stock. Check the numbers against the stock records. If any are different, look at all the movement slips for the item, and try to find out where the error arose!

● Discuss the levels to which the stock should be allowed to drop before more stock is ordered. Also discuss the quantities which should be re-ordered. Check the amount of space available for each item in the cupboard!

QUESTIONS

1 Look at the way you set out the stock records and movement slips. After you have run the system for a while, do you think that any fields in them are unnecessary? Would you like to have included any additional fields? For example, would it be useful to include the stock levels before and after each movement on the movement slip?

Comment on your answers.

2 If the stock level on a stock record did not agree with the number in stock when you counted it, how easy was it to find out where the mistake had occurred?

Comment on your answer.

3 Select an item of stock for which you have a number of movement records. Draw a graph of the number in stock against the date (or the time, if you simulated a number of movements in the same day).

Look carefully at the graph, and estimate from it the average rate at which the stock is removed. For example, if 120 items were removed over ten days, then the average rate is twelve items per day. This means that if it takes five days for a new order to arrive, the minimum stock level is 60 books.

a) Use this information to suggest a suitable minimum stock level, and re-order quantity.

b) Repeat this process for other stock items.

5.3 Check Digits

Items in a stock control system are identified by **item numbers**. Each item has its own number, which is used to locate its record in the stock file. It is very important that mistakes are not made with item numbers, otherwise stock movements can be entered on the wrong records.

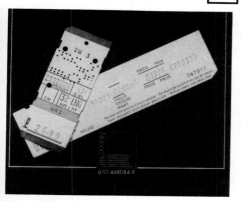

Two examples of check digits on a book — the International Standard Book Number (ISBN) has one check digit, and the price label has another.

To help prevent errors, most stock control systems have one or more **check digits** on item numbers. These are extra letters or digits, on the end of item numbers. They can be worked out from the other digits in the number.

When an item number is typed at the keyboard, or read from a bar code, the check digit is input as part of the number. The computer then works out what the check digit should be, from the rest of the item number. It compares this with the check digit entered. If the two do not match, then the item number (or the check digit) has been entered wrongly.

There are many methods of working out check digits. A simple one is to add up the odd digits of the item number, and also add up the even digits. The difference between the totals is the check digit. For example:

Item number: 3428

Odd digits: 3 + 2 = 5

Even digits: 4 + 8 = 12

Difference: 12 − 5 = 7

The check digit is 7. The item number with its check digit is 34287.

Check digits are used with item numbers in stock control systems. They are also used with bank account numbers and credit card numbers. They are very useful whenever a number is used for identification, and when a mistake in the number could cause serious problems.

Other methods of calculating check digits are included in the exercise at the end of this chapter.

QUESTIONS

1 List some uses for check digits. Include those mentioned in the text, and others you know about.

2 Why are check digits important?

3 Work out the check digits on the following numbers, using the above method:

5914   5194   231342   231432

Look carefully at the differences between the numbers, and comment on your answers.

5.4 Small Business Stock Control

This activity is best suited to a group of between three and five pupils. It can be done either on a computer, or using a stock card system. It can form the basis of an extended project.

Choose a suitable small business such as a clothes shop, car parts shop, garden centre or sports shop. Use a local business directory to help you. Think very carefully about the kind of stock the business would have. If possible, visit a nearby business like the one you have chosen to get a better idea.

- Decide on a suitable method of allocating stock numbers. You may want to group the goods by colours or sizes.

- Devise a simple system of check digits for the stock numbers.

- Decide what information to include in the stock records. This may include the name and address of the supplier. You may also wish to include the cost price of the goods, and the selling price.

- For each item, decide on a minimum stock level and the amount to order when the stock falls below this level.

- Now enter a set of stock records, one for each item you wish to include in the business. Work out the check digit for each item number. Include a suitable stock level to start with.

- Design the slips to record each movement of stock. Decide what information to include, and how to set it out.

- Now carry out a series of imaginary stock movements. Let some members of the group fill in movement slips, and others look up the stock records and adjust the stock levels. One or two members can be in charge of checking stock levels and writing out orders for more stock.

- After enough stock movements have been recorded, discuss how well your stock control system has worked.

QUESTIONS

1 Did you include the right kinds of information on –
   a) the stock records?
   b) the movement slips?
   Comment on your answers.

2 Select one item in your stock control system. Find all the movement records for the item. Starting with the initial stock level, use the movement records to check the final stock level for the item. Does it match the final stock level in the stock record for the item? If not, try to find out where the mistake has occurred, and comment on your findings.

3 Comment on how well your system of check digits worked.

5.5 Computer Elements: Bar Codes and Magnetic Strips

Bar codes are used to identify many items sold in shops and supermarkets. They consist of a pattern of wide and narrow stripes which represents a number. The number is printed below the bars. It includes a check digit. Each type of item has its own number on the bar code.

Bar code readers scan the pattern of bars, and read the code into a computer. They are most often used with **point-of-sale terminals** at supermarket checkouts. Some bar code readers look like pens — they are passed across the bars to read them. Others have windows against which the goods are held for the bar code to be read. Both types check the code as it is read. The pens make a sound when they have read the code — if no sound is made, the code must be read again. The other type reads the code repeatedly until it is input correctly. A number of checks are carried out. These include the use of check digits.

Magnetic strips are used on the price tags of goods in many shops. They can hold more information than bar codes. They contain the code number of the article, and may have other information such as its size and colour. They may also have the date when the article was put on sale. Magnetic strips are read by a device which looks like a pen, attached to the point-of-sale terminal in the shop. It works in a similar way to a pen-type bar code reader.

Bar codes and magnetic strips save a lot of time. The information on them can be read quickly, and errors in reading it are rare. They help customers to be served quickly, and keep the number of mistakes in recording sales to a minimum.

A bar code being read at a record library.

A price tag which includes a magnetic strip. This holds the price, stock number and other information.

A magnetic strip being read at a point-of-sale terminal.

QUESTIONS

1 What is the advantage of a magnetic strip over a bar code? What it its disadvantage?

2 What are the benefits of the use of bar codes and magnetic strips?

3 What happens if a bar code or magnetic strip is read wrongly?

5.6 Stock Control in Practice

A bar code reader being used to read a person's library card.

Computers are becoming increasingly popular for stock control. Point-of-sale systems are common in most large shops, and computers are used in the warehouses which supply these shops. Many factories are installing computers for stock control in their parts warehouses. Gas, water and electricity boards use computers to manage the large numbers of parts they need for their work. The computer systems which most libraries use to record the loan of books are very similar to stock control systems.

Stock control systems are often part of larger computer systems. In shops, they are part of the system which records sales. Sales are entered at the point-of-sale terminals, which produce a record of each sale. This includes the date, time, items sold and the money received. The information about the items sold is used to bring the stock records up-to-date. The information about the money is used to bring the company's accounts up-to-date.

The use of computers for stock control is helping to make companies much more efficient. Shops can adjust stock levels finely, so that they do not run out of stock, but levels are as low as possible. This saves money and helps to keep prices down. It also helps to ensure that perishable goods such as foods are not wasted by being kept too long in warehouses. Companies which use large numbers of components can reduce their stock levels to as little as one day's supply. This saves large sums of money, and means that big warehouses are not necessary.

QUESTIONS

1 List some places in which computers are used for stock control. Include places mentioned in the text, and others which you know about.

2 What are the advantages of using computers for stock control?

3 How are stock control systems linked to other computer systems?

Going Out of Business

● It is the last day of the closing down sale at Cloud 9 Fashions. The shop has been losing money for months. It has been bought by the Chic chain, which has clothes shops all over Europe.

Belinda Smith, the manager of Cloud 9 Fashions, has been employed by the new owners. She will manage the new branch of Chic when it opens. Michelle Hugo, the area manageress for Chic, is explaining how things will be different when the new shop opens.

Michelle: You will have a sales terminal at the desk. Each garment has a magnetic strip on the price tag. This has the code number for the garment, its size, colour combination, cost price, and the date it was delivered to the shop. When you sell a garment, the information on the tag is read at the terminal. It is stored on a cassette tape.

Belinda: Why do you need all that information? We never used to keep it at Cloud 9.

Michelle: It is very important to know how fast clothes are selling. If a type of garment is selling slowly, we reduce the price to clear the stock.

Belinda: Do you change the price for each branch separately?

Michelle: No, our computer collects the information from the sales termninal in each branch every evening. Sales are then analysed by regions. When a garment is selling slowly in a region, its price is changed for all the shops in the region.

Belinda: Why do you need to know the colours of the garments which are sold?

Michelle: All the garments we sell are colour co-ordinated. If one colour is becoming more popular, we need to order more skirts, blouses, scarves and shoes in that colour from the factories.

Belinda: How soon can you do this?

Michelle: The computer analyses sales by colour every night. Orders can be placed the day after a trend is noticed. We can have more stock in the shops within five days. The distribution is all planned by computer.

Belinda: We never did things like that at Cloud 9 . . .

QUESTIONS

1 a) List two benefits of the computerised stock control system which are mentioned in the story.
b) Suggest some further benefits.

2 Why is it important to know how long a garment has been in a shop before it is sold?

3 Fashions are sometimes changed overnight by a celebrity wearing something striking on television. Suggest how the computer system in a chain of clothes shops could be used to confirm that a demand for the item does exist, and plan the ordering and distribution of the new garment.

4 Make a list of all the reasons you can deduce from the story for Cloud 9 Fashions going out of business. Also make a list of the reasons for the Chic chain of shops being able to extend throughout Europe.

Exercise 5

1 Write down the meanings of the following words or phrases: card index, file, record, field, minimum stock level, re-order quantity, movement record, bar code, check digit, cash terminal.

2 Work out the check digits for the following numbers, using the method from Section 5.3:

7613   7163   1673   7316

243586   245386   253486   248536

Comment on your answers.

3 Set up stock control systems similar to those described in the activities in Sections 5.2 and 5.4 for any of the following:
a) a stamp collection;
b) the contents of a freezer;
c) the canteen at a youth club;
d) the parts kept by a plumber or electrician.

4 An alternative method of working out check digits is to multiply each digit in a number by a **weighting factor**, add up the products and take the last digit of the sum. For example, using the weighting factors 1, 3, 5 and 7 on the number 9428:

Number:	9	4	2	8	
Weighting factors:	$\times 7$	$\times 5$	$\times 3$	$\times 1$	
Products:	63	$+ 20$	$+ 6$	$+ 8$	$= 97$

The check digit is 7.

Work out the check digits for the first four numbers in Question 2 by this method. Compare them with those obtained by the previous method.

Comment on your answers.

Things to Find Out

1 Find out if any shops or businesses near your school use computers for their stock control. If so, find out what benefits the systems have brought, and if there have been any problems.

2 Find out as many uses as you can for check digits. Make a list of them, and state why each is important.

3 Find out some uses for bar codes in addition to those mentioned in the text. For each one, state why bar codes are particularly suitable.

Points to Discuss

1 Computers have made it possible to keep much more careful control over stocks of goods. Many of the benefits of this are mentioned in the text.

Make a list of all the benefits of more careful stock control. Discuss the importance of each one, both for the organisation which keeps the stock, and for its customers.

2 It is possible that some supermarkets may be replaced by warehouses, with goods ordered by customers using home computers. The warehouses will be controlled entirely by computers, which will instruct robots to make up each order. They will also keep records of stock, and order items when necessary. Very few staff will be employed.

Discuss the advantages and disadvantages of this type of shopping:
a) for customers;
b) for the companies which own the supermarkets;
c) for the people who work at supermarkets.

3 As described in Section 5.7, many small shops are being taken over by large chains of shops which use computers. Discuss the advantages and disadvantages of these takeovers for –
a) the customers;
b) the people who work at the shops.

4 Many countries in the Third World suffer severe food shortages. These are caused partly by poor harvests, and partly by very inefficient methods of storing and distributing food. Much of the food rots, or is eaten by insects and animals, while it is being stored in warehouses.

Look at newspaper articles and other reports of a recent famine, and try to find out the reasons for the shortage of food.

Discuss the benefits of using computers for stock control in these countries. Also discuss the difficulties in implementing such systems, and any problems which they could cause.

6.

Tables of numbers

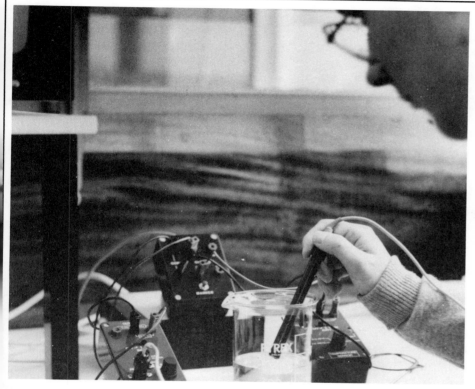

● Dr James Macintosh was very tired. It was three o'clock in the morning, and he would need at least another two hours before he could finish recording his experiment. It had already been running for ten hours.

The experiment was testing the effects of a new drug on cancer cells. He had made a culture of the cells, and administered the drug. Every two minutes, he used some electronic equipment to measure what was happening to the cells. He wrote the results down in his notebook.

The time between taking measurements was not long enough to do anything else, not even to make a cup of coffee. He was trying to read an article, but he could not concentrate properly.

Finally he was finished. He packed up very carefully and went home. He took most of the morning off to recover.

When he returned to work in the afternoon, he copied all his results into a table, and set to work with his calculator. He frequently made mistakes because he was tired. He did most calculations three times to be sure that there were no errors.

After several hours, he had a graph of his results. They showed that the drug was having some effect, but not very much. He would have to repeat the experiment under slightly different conditions. That would have to wait for another day. He was under pressure to get a result from his experiment, but he could not face another night in the laboratory.

QUESTIONS

1 What two tasks took so much of Dr Macintosh's time?

2 What equipment was he using to produce his results?

3 Dr Macintosh is a qualified medical scientist. Do you think that the tasks he was doing were making the best use of his skills?

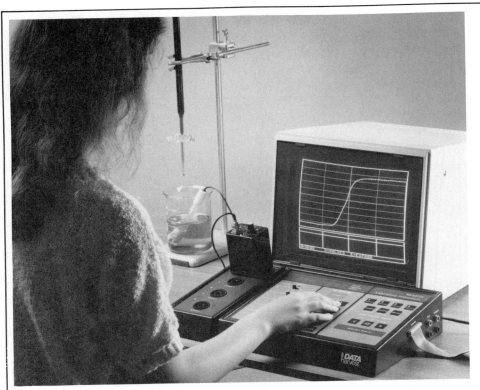

● In another laboratory, Dr Shiela Scott was setting up an experiment. The aim was to measure the rate at which various substances are absorbed by certain cells. The result could help explain why some babies are born prematurely, and would be very helpful in the treatment of severe burns.

Dr Scott prepared a culture of the cells. She carefully measured the quantities of the substances she wished to test. She poured the substances into the culture.

She then set up the automatic measuring equipment for the experiment. She placed the probes in the culture, and set the time interval between measurements — two minutes. She checked the first two measurements as they were made. After

half an hour, she checked the experiment again. She spent the rest of the afternoon on other work, and checked the apparatus again before she went home.

When she came into the laboratory the next morning, the experiment was still running. She looked at the results that were coming in, and decided to leave it for one more hour. She then stopped the experiment, and cleared up very carefully.

Dr Scott connected the measuring equipment to the computer on her desk. She transferred all the results to the computer and stored them on a disk. She made a second copy of the disk just to be safe.

She then used a computer program to analyse the results. She instructed the computer to perform certain

calculations, and then to plot a graph on the screen. She checked the formulae that she had entered, to be sure that the calculations were being done correctly. When she was satisfied, she stored the results on disk, and printed a copy of the graph.

The results were interesting, but not conclusive. She needed to repeat the whole experiment at a slightly higher temperature, to see what difference it would make if a person had a fever. She made a new tissue culture, and set the experiment running again.

While the experiment was running, an idea occurred to her. She ran her computer program again, and called up the results. This time she carried out a slightly different set of calculations. The results were much more significant...

QUESTIONS

1 In what **two** ways did Dr Scott work differently from Dr Macintosh?

2 How did the two scientist check their calculations? How likely were there to be errors in the results?

3 Did Dr Scott's work tire her out? Suggest some consequences of this for the results she was getting.

4 Was Dr Scott making the best use of her time in the laboratory? Comment on the your answer.

6.1 Computer Programs Which Process Results

One of the oldest uses of computers is to store the results of experiments, and do calculations on these figures. In the early days, scientists had to write their own programs for these tasks. Today there are many programs available which can be used for these purposes. Some research workers use these programs as they are; others modify them to suit their own needs. Others continue to write their own programs.

Most programs which process results store the information in large **tables**. The tables have one column for each quantity measured, such as time and temperature, and one row for each result. Most can store hundreds or even thousands of results.

The numbers can be typed into the tables, or they can be loaded directly from measuring equipment, as described in the previous section. Once it is in a table, the information can be saved on disk and printed. A table on disk can be read into memory at any time, and the numbers processed further.

The information can be processed in a variety of ways. The person using the program gives instructions to the computer to carry out the operations which are needed. For example, the program can be made to calculate the total and the average of the numbers in a column. It can plot a graph of the numbers in one column against those in another. If one column has a set of distances, and another a set of times, a formula can be entered to calculate a set of speeds in a third column. The frequencies of the numbers in a column can be added up, and a histogram drawn of the results.

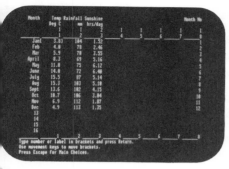

Temperature, rainfall and sunshine figures in a table, ready to be processed by computer.

QUESTIONS

1 In what form are results stored for processing?

2 How often can results be processed, once they have been stored on disk?

3 List **five** ways in which experimental results can be processed.

ACTIVITY 6.2 Pulse Rate Experiment

The aim of this activity is to measure the pulse rates of all the pupils in a class. The results are recorded, and a histogram is drawn of them. It is best carried out as a class activity.

First make sure that you can all take your pulse!

Get someone to call out the start and end of a minute, and count the number of heartbeats during the minute. Choose a member of the class to enter and analyse the results.

- Start the program which analyses tables of numbers. Look at the instructions for the use of the program to find out how to carry out the steps described below.

- Open up a blank table. Give the table a suitable heading, and head three columns as follows:

Pulse Rate (Beat/min)	Interval (Beat/min)	Frequency

The second row gives the units of measurement in the column.

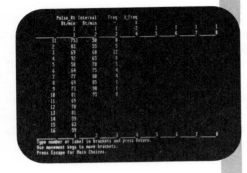

- Let each pupil call out the number of heartbeats that he or she counted. This is the pulse rate in beats per minute. The pupil at the computer types these numbers into the first column.

- Use the program to calculate the **mean** of the numbers. This is the average pulse rate for the class.

- Use the program to sort the numbers in ascending order. This shows the smallest to the largest pulse rate.

- Count the **frequencies** of the pulse rates in suitable intervals:

  Use the second column for the intervals. A suitable range might be from 50 to 100 beats per minute, in steps of 10. The first interval is 50 to 59 beats per minute, the second 60 to 69, and so on.

  Use the third column for the frequencies. The first frequency is the number of pupils with pulse rates between 50 and 59 beats per minute.

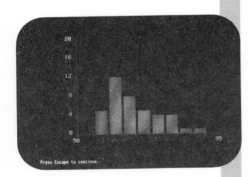

- Display a **histogram** of the frequencies: plot a bar graph of the frequencies as the y-axis, against the intervals as the x-axis.

  There should be a 'hump' in the middle of the range, showing that most of the pulse rates are grouped in this region. There may be a smaller 'hump' at the low end of the range. Find out why this could occur.

- Save all the results on disk, and print them if required.

Variations

1 Do the activity as above, but enter the pulse rates for the boys and those for the girls in separate columns. Count the frequencies for the boys and girls separately, but using the same intervals. Compare the two histograms and comment on any differences.

2 Get everyone in the class to raise their arms above their heads twenty times, and then measure the pulse rates again. Comment on the differences in the results.

● **A C T I V I T Y**   6.3 **Weather Records**

The automatic weather recording instrument sent up with a weather balloon.

The aim of this activity is to measure changes in the weather over a suitable period of time. The weather can be recorded each day for a week or month, or every quarter of an hour during a single day.

First decide what weather readings you are going to take. This depends on your source of information. You may have weather recording instruments at the school. If not, most newspapers carry weather reports for each day. Use the library to find these reports over a suitable period of time. The Prestel service also carries weather reports (see Chapter 8).

The usual weather measurements are the temperature, amount of rainfall, hours of sunshine, relative humidity, wind speed and direction. The temperature may be the average over the interval, or the maximum and minimum temperatures during the period.

● Make a table of the results. Use the left-hand column for the date or time, and the other columns for the measurements. Choose suitable number codes for the dates and wind directions.

● Run the program on your school's computer which stores and analyses results. Open up a blank table, and head the columns in it something like this:

Date	Max Temp Deg C	Min Temp Deg C	Rainfall mm	Sunshine hours	Humidity %	WindSpd m/sec	WindDir

● Type your results into the table. Check them carefully, and correct any errors.

● Calculate the average in each column. Look at the figures, and see by how much they vary from the average. Comment on the variation.

● Plot a line or bar graph of each figure as the y-axis, against the time or date as the x-axis. These graphs show how the figures varied over the time of the survey. Comment on this variation.

- Plot scattergaphs of various pairs of figures. For example, plot rainfall against sunshine. You would expect there to be more rain with less sun. Do your results show this trend?

- Save your results on disk, and print them if necessary.

QUESTIONS

1 Look at satellite photographs or weather maps of the area taken during your survey. Discuss the results with reference to these maps or photographs.

2 Is there a relationship between any two of the quantities you measured in your survey? If so, explain how you think it comes about.

3 Make a list of any possible sources of error in your results. Check each source carefully, and comment on your findings.

● **ACTIVITY**   6.4 **Height and Weight**

The aim of this activity is to investigate the increase in height and weight of pupils as they get older. It is best done by groups of between three and five pupils.

- Measure the height and weight of as many pupils as you can. Also record the age (in years and months) of each pupil. Try to get as wide a range of ages as you can.

- Convert the ages to years and decimals of a year. For example, 14 years and 3 months is 14.25 years.

- Set out your results in a table as follows, with the boys and girls separately:

Girls	Age Years	Height mm	Weight kg	Boys	Age Years	Height mm	Weight kg

- Run the program on your school's computer which analyses experimental results. Open up a new table, and enter headings and units as above.

- Enter the measurements you have made into the columns. (The columns headed **Girls** and **Boys** are blank.) Check the numbers carefully, and correct any mistakes.

- Get the computer to work out the averages of the columns. These show the average height, weight and age of the girls and boys you have measured. Comment on the figures.

- Plot scattergraphs of the heights and weights against the ages. The first graph has the girls' age as the x-axis and their height as the y-axis. These show how heights and weights change as pupils get older.

  Look carefully at the graphs. Are the points grouped around a line? Can you estimate by how much the height or weight changes in a year? If so, write down these changes in the heights and weights, and comment on them.

- Plot a scattergraph of the height as the x-axis and the weight as the y-axis. Make one graph for the boys, and one graph for the girls. These graphs show whether there is a relationship between height and weight.

  Look carefully at the graphs. If the points are grouped around a line, then there is a definite relationship between height and weight. Is this the case for your results? If there is a relationship between height and weight, can you see what it is? Are the taller pupils also the heavier ones?

  Comment on the differences between the results for the boys and those for the girls.

- Save your results on disk, and print them.

QUESTIONS

1 How useful was the computer for storing and analysing your results?

2 Make a list of all the places where you could have made mistakes when analysing your results on the computer. Check them carefully, and comment on whether you did find any mistakes.

  Now make a list of all the ways you could have made mistakes if you had done all the work on paper. Comment on the differences between these and the sources of error on the computer.

A probe which measures the acidity of a liquid.

6.5 Computer Elements: Automatic Sensors

Many computers used for laboratory work are connected directly to measuring equipment. There are **probes** which measure temperature and pressure, the flow of electric currents, and many similar quantities.

The information recorded by the probes is not in the same form as that stored and processed by computer. It is in **analogue** form — the probe returns a **voltage** which is proportional to the quantity being measured. A conversion device changes the analogue signal (the voltage) to the **digital** form used by the computer. The signals are **sampled** at regular intervals.

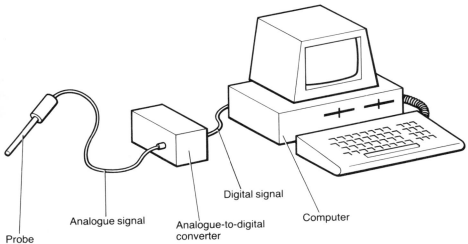

Figure 6.1: Analogue and digital signals

A digital-to-analogue converter.

Many microcomputers contain **analogue-to-digital conversion (ADC)** devices of this sort. They can be programmed to sample the signals from a probe, and convert the voltages into digital quantities. Other labratory systems use measuring equipment which takes the samples, and converts and stores them. The measurements are later transferred to the computer, in one operation. (The **Vela** measuring device works in this fashion.)

Using automatic measuring devices has many advantages. It means that experiments can be set up and then left to run by themselves. Measurements can be taken very quickly — thousands of times per second if necessary. It also means that measurements can be taken in places which are difficult to reach. For example, automatic measuring equipment can be sent up in weather balloons and satellites. Remote lighthouses, lightships and bouys can take weather readings automatically. Small probes can be inserted into people's bodies, and sometimes left there for weeks. Probes can operate inside dangerous environments like nuclear reactors.

The use of automatic measuring equipment has made many experiments possible which could not have been done without them. Many advances in medicine and space research, for example, would have not been made if they were not available.

QUESTIONS

1 List some advantages of automatic measuring devices. Include those mentioned in the text, and others you can think of.

2 How is information transferred between measuring devices and computers?

3 List some uses of automatic measuring devices. Include those in the text, and others you know about.

6.6 Processing Experimental Results in Practice

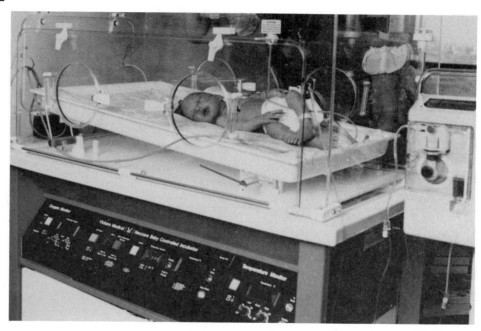

A Vickers incubator in use at Guy's Hospital. The temperature and oxygen level in the incubator are monitored automatically.

An item of automatic test equipment made by Smiths Industries, being tested.

Electronic measuring equipment and computers to analyse results are used very widely. They are used for research work at universities and in industry. Almost all experiments in science, engineering and medicine are done with the aid of automatic measuring equipment and computers. Research laboratories in chemical plants and factories which make medicines use them extensively.

Automatic test equipment is used in industry to check products. For example, motor cars undergo hundreds of checks before they leave the factory. Many of these are computerised. The testing of aircraft and aircraft engines is even more thorough. The flow of oil and gas from production platforms in the North Sea is constantly monitored by automatic equipment. The operation of nuclear power stations is checked all the time, and measurements are stored for investigation by computer.

Hospitals are making increasing use of electronic equipment to keep checks on the condition of patients. Babies born prematurely have their breathing, heartbeat and the oxygen levels in their blood monitored continuously. People who have had serious accidents, heart attacks or strokes have similar monitors. In some hospitals, the readings taken by the monitoring equipment are transferred to computers for analysis.

Computers are used to process the results of opinion surveys. They are also used for census work. This is one of the oldest applications of automatic computers, dating back nearly a century.

QUESTIONS

1 What are the benefits of using computers for census work?

2 a) Describe some of the ways in which computers are used in hospitals.
   b) Suggest come future uses for computers in hospitals.

3 Suggest some reasons for keeping careful checks on the operation of nuclear power stations.

Exercise 6

1 Write down the meanings of the following terms: automatic test equipment, monitor, analogue, digital, sample.

2 Conventional clocks and watches, sundials and mercury thermometers are analogue devices. Car mileage indicators are digital devices. Make lists of other analogue and digital devices.

Use the steps described in Sections 6.2, 6.3 and 6.4 for each of the following activities. They are suitable for groups of between three and five pupils, and may form the basis of extended projects.

3 Enter some tables of census information for your local area. If possible, get a set of figures for your local area, and a corresponding set from an area of similar size in another part of the country. Choose suitable factors to investigate, such as the size of families, or the number of cars per household. Use the school library or the local library to find the census tables.

Enter one or more tables of the information. The usual layout is as follows (the example shows the numbers of households with various numbers of cars in the household):

Area	Total Households	No Car Households	One Car Households	Two Cars Households	More Cars Households
Area 1	....				
Area 2	....				
....					

The units of measurement are households. The names of the areas are entered in the left column.

The areas are either **enumeration districts**, which are only a few blocks, or **wards**, which are larger. Draw a sketch map of the areas you have included.

Calculate the totals and averages in each column, and comment on them. For example, is there a relationship between the availability of public transport and the number of cars?

Draw bar graphs of the various columns against the areas. These show how the figures vary from one area to another. Comment on these variations.

Plot scattergrams of different columns against each other. If the points are grouped around a line, it means that there is some relationship between the quantities. If so, state what the relationship is, and suggest reasons for it.

4 If you have any probes which can measure quantities such as temperature or light intensity, and a way of passing the measurements to your school's computer, there are a number of experiments which can be done. Here are some ideas:

a) The heating system of your school is probably set to give a certain temperature throughout the school. Select a classroom which is used by different groups of pupils throughout the day, and which is empty for some of the day. Set up a temperature probe and a computer in the classroom, to measure the temperature at suitable intervals throughout the day. Transfer the results into a table, and plot a graph of temperature against time. How close is the actual temperature to that which is set? Suggest reasons for the variations. (If the heating is not switched on, this experiment will measure the variations in temperature caused by the presence of different numbers of people in the room.)

b) Measure the variation in temperature outside the school building over a whole day. If possible, set the equipment to run for 24 hours. Transfer the results into a table, and plot a graph of temperature against time. This shows the range of temperatures a building must cope with during a day. Comment on the problems caused by this variation.

5 Use newspapers to find weather reports from other countries. Alternatively use tables from the Meteorological Office for weather figures from different parts of Britain in the past.

Enter tables of these figures, as described in Section 6.3 Analyse the information as described in that section. Look carefully at the similarities and differences between these results and those for your own area. Comment on these.

Things to Find Out

1 Find out how mechanical computers were used to record and analyse census results in the United States of America in 1890. What improvements did they bring over previous methods? How have methods of analysing census results changed since then?

2 Find out if there are any colleges, factories or industrial laboratories near your school which use automatic sensing or testing equipment, or which use computers to process experimental results. If so, find out what equipment is used, and what the advantages are of its use.

Points to Discuss

1 Make a list of serious medical problems which are unsolved. A cure for cancer is one item on this list. For each of these problems, discuss ways in which computers can be used to help to solve them.

2 In the last ten years, computers, robots and automatic test equipment have been used extensively in the making of motor cars. Discuss whether these have led to an improvement in the quality of motor cars over this period. Do you think that this has helped to make roads safer?

3 Processing tables of numbers ('number crunching' as it is called) is one of the oldest uses of computers. Today it is only one among the many uses of computers. The most common use of computers at present is for word processing. Discuss this change in the use of computers away from number crunching. Has it improved the image of computers in the eyes of the public?

7.

Drawings and designs

● Steven Jones works for a firm of architects. He and some colleagues are busy preparing drawings to bid for a large contract. The contract is for an art gallery in the centre of a town. They have drawn a **plan** of the building (looked at from above), and a number of **elevations**, showing how it looks from the front and from each side.

On the morning of the day when the bid must be sent in, Steven and his colleagues have a meeting. They review the drawings, and decide that one more is needed. They ask Steven to produce a drawing which shows how the building will look as a person walks across the square in front of it. The drawing is from an angle, and has to be in **perspective**, showing distant parts of the building smaller than those at the front.

Steven sets to work at his drawing board. He uses the plan and elevations of the building as the basis of his drawing. He works out the angles with his calculator. After several hours, he has the main outline complete. He realises that some features of the building are going to look rather awkward from the angle of his drawing. He calls his colleagues to look.

After some discussion, they decide that a few small changes to the design will make the building look much better. They return to their drawing boards and make the changes on the plan and elevations. Steven then transfers these changes to his

drawing and looks at the effect. His colleagues agree that the new design is a great improvement. Steven just manages to finish his drawing by the end of the afternoon. The company's bid for the work of designing the art gallery is now complete.

• At another firm of architects, Katie Black and her colleagues are working on a design for the same art gallery. Their company is also going to bid for the contract. They have entered the basic outline of the building into the **computer-aided design (CAD)** system which they use for all their designs.

This outline is in three dimensions. It can be rotated by the computer to produce plans and elevations, and perspective views. These are displayed on the screen, and may be enlarged to any size.

Any view of the design can be printed.

Katie rotates the design on the screen. She and her colleagues look at it very carefully from all angles. They make slight changes to the outline, until they are satisfied with its appearance. Katie call up a detailed design for the windows, which is already stored in the CAD system. She inserts it into all the windows, and looks at the result. Her colleagues do not like it, and she calls up another window design instead. Katie makes some slight changes to this

design, and copies them to all the windows in the building. After a few minutes, they are all happy with the design.

Katie adds a few more details, and sketches in the trees in the square in front of the building. She calls up a sequence of perspective views. These show how the appearance of the building changes as a person walks across the square towards the main entrance. Katie and her colleagues decide to use this sequence of views an an introduction to their presentation. They connect the computer screen to a video recorder, and make a short video film of the sequence.

Katie selects the views needed for printed plans, and instructs the computer to print them. Her company's bid is now ready to be sent in.

QUESTIONS

1 What types of drawings are:
a) a plan?
b) an elevation?
c) a perspective view?

2 In the first story, at what stage did it become apparent that there was a fault in the design of the building? How was the design corrected?

3 In the second story, how were modifications made to the design of the building?

4 Which company was able to make a more attractive presentation of their design? Is this likely to affect their chances of getting the contract to design the art gallery?

Comment on your answers.

7.1 A Computer-Aided Design System

The outside of the Louvre gallery, shown on a Computer Vision CAD system. The outline of the proposed new entrance is drawn, to show its effect on the existing building.

Computer-aided design systems are replacing the use of drawing boards for preparing architect's and engineer's drawings. They are also used for the designs of microchips and printed circuit boards used by computers. They are coming into use for all types of design work, including film and television production.

Some CAD systems can be used to test designs, and calculate the quantities of materials needed to build the designs. Others are linked directly to manufacturing equipment. This enables the designs to be constructed automatically by computer-controlled machines and robots. This chapter, however, concentrates on the drawing facilities of CAD systems.

CAD systems use a variety of special hardware, but they can all do the same kinds of things. They all have some method of drawing onto the computer screen. This might be with the aid of a **light pen**, which draws directly on the screen, or a **digitising pad** which moves on a flat surface, and produces images on the screen. Straight and curved lines of varying widths can be drawn. Areas can be shaded, in colour in some systems. Text can be entered via the keyboard, to label the drawings.

Many CAD systems work in three dimensions. A flat drawing is entered first, either a plan or an elevation. This is then tilted so that the third dimension can be drawn in. The image can be enlarged, reduced, rotated and stretched as often as required. Portions of a drawing can be 'cut out' and 'pasted in' somewhere else. The image can be saved on disk at any time, and any view of it can be printed.

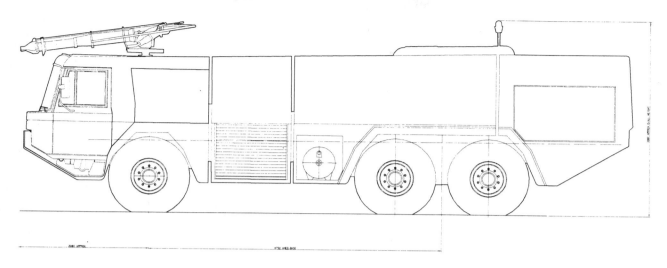

A new design for a fire engine, on a CAD system.

A **library** of design elements can be built up. For example, a bridge may require a large number of joints, all of which are the same. The joint is designed once and stored in the library. It is then called up and inserted at each point where it is required. This saves hours of repetitive drafting to make all the copies.

QUESTIONS

1 How are drawings entered into a CAD system?

2 What can be done to a design, once it has been entered, in a CAD system?

3 How can a CAD system save time?

● **ACTIVITY**

7.2 A Kitchen Plan

The aim of this activity is to produce a design for the layout of a kitchen. It can be a new design for the kitchen in your house, or your idea of an ideal kitchen.

Before you start using the computer, make a list of all the things which are to be done in the kitchen. For example, will any meals be eaten there? Does there need to be a place to put out food for a cat or a dog? Decide how many people will work in the kitchen at one time.

Then make a list of all the units you need in the kitchen. Decide whether to include things like a freezer and a dishwasher.

When your lists are complete, start up the computer-aided design program on your school's computer. Look at the instruction book for the program to find out how to do the various tasks. You are going to draw a **plan** (a view from above) of the kitchen.

- Start with a blank screen, and enter the outline of the walls of the kitchen. Use a suitable scale, such as two centimetres to one metre.

- Mark the windows and doors, and draw semicircles to show how the doors swing open.

- It is a good idea to save this outline on disk, so that you can call it up if you want to start a new design.

- Try out various positions for the units on your list. Draw outlines of them only, making estimates of their size. Make the best use of the light coming in through the windows. Think carefully how easy it will be to reach various units.

- When the units are all in place, draw in the worktops, cupboards and tables you need. Finish your design by adding electric sockets and lights, and, if you have time, draw the pattern of the tiles on the floor!

- Save your complete design on disk and print it.

QUESTIONS

1 Follow the moves needed by a person to make a cup of tea in the kitchen you have designed. Do they have to walk further than necessary?

2 If one person is doing the washing up, and another is drying, will they get in each other's way? If so, suggest some improvements to the design.

3 Make a list of all the things in your kitchen, and estimate or find out the cost of each one. Work out the total cost. (You may wish to use a spreadsheet for this.)

● ACTIVITY

7.3 Design a Set for a School Play

The aim of this activity is to use the school's CAD system to design a set for a school play. It is suitable for a group of between three and five pupils. It may form the basis of an extended project.

If your school is not putting on a play at present, choose a play which you would like to be produced. If a play is being produced, find out which one it is. Get advice from the teachers who are putting on the play. Your set design might even be the one they use!

- Read through the play, and make a list of the scenes. Group them into scenes which can be played on the same set.

- You may find that you can use the same set for the whole play. If not, keep the number of changes of set to a minimum. You may be able to make small changes to the set to create different scenes.

- Make rough sketches of the school stage — a plan and the elevation as seen from the audience. Put in the approximate dimensions, and include the curtains.

- Enter the plan and elevation of the stage onto the CAD program on the school computer system. Choose a suitable scale. Save the drawings on disk. These two drawings can be the basis of the set designs.

- Now decide on an overall theme for the set. Keep it simple, but make it as dramatic as possible! Having several levels on the set often makes it more interesting, and gives the players more scope.

  Most stage scenery is made from flat sections joined together by hinges. This makes it easy to store when it is not in use. Raised portions can be created by piling up boxes of various shapes.

- Call up the stage plan, and draw the plan of each set. Save each plan and print it.

- Draw the elevation of each flat section as viewed from directly in front of it. Then rotate the image to show the section as it would be viewed by the audience.

- When you are happy with the overall outline of each flat section, colour it in. Try various colour combinations.

- Combine the elevations of the separate flat sections into a single drawing of each set, looked at by someone in the audience. If possible, alter the perspective to show it from each side of the hall.

- Save all the drawings on disk, and print them.

Part of the stage set for 'Starlight Express'. The set consists of a number of high-speed roller skating ramps, some of which go right round the back of the audience.

QUESTIONS

1 Think how you would have done the same designs if you were using pencil and paper. Make a list of the advantages and disadvantages of the CAD system.

2 How would you be able to find out what a stage set looks like from various parts of the hall without using a CAD system?

3 If there is more than one set for the play, how easy is it going to be to change sets? Can the CAD system help you to plan these changes? If so, suggest how this can be done.

● **A C T I V I T Y**

7.4 Design Colour Schemes for a Ship, Train or Aircraft

The way a ship, train or aircraft is painted is very important. A good colour scheme makes it more attractive to passengers. Airlines spend a lot of money on the colour schemes for their planes — they believe that better colours mean more passengers!

In this activity you will design alternative colour schemes for a ship, train or aircraft. The aim is to produce a colour scheme which is as attractive as possible.

- Look at some photographs of ships, planes and trains to get some ideas. Note the use of stripes - they can make something look longer and thinner! See how the names or symbols of shipping companies, railways or airlines are included in the colour schemes.

- Decide whether you are going to design the colour scheme for a ship, train or aircraft. Draw an outline of the one you have chosen on the CAD system on your school's computer. A view from the side is sufficient, though you may include a view from above if you wish. (If your CAD system is not in colour, choose patterns to represent colours. If it is in three dimensions, draw a three-dimensional view, but keep it very simple.)

- Save the outline on disk. Call up the outline when you start each colour scheme. Make sure that you do not over-write it with a coloured-in drawing.

- Now try a colour scheme. Draw the outlines of the areas to be coloured, and then fill them with colour. Include letters or symbols for the name of the shipping company, airline or railway.

- Each time you are satisfied with a colour scheme, save it on disk. Call up the original outline to start the next design. Continue in this way until you have five or six colour schemes.

- Print each colour scheme. If your printer is not in colour, colour in the shaded patterns by hand.

QUESTIONS

1 Conduct a survey of your friends, getting them to vote for their favourite colour scheme. Add up the votes, and sort the schemes in order of popularity.

Why do you think that this order was chosen?

2 What are the benefits to an airline of trying out colour schemes for its planes on a CAD system, rather than painting a number of models?

3 Suggest a colour scheme for a ship, train or aircraft which would put you off travelling in it. (How about black all over?) Discuss the reasons for some colour schemes being more attractive than others.

7.5 Computer Elements: Light Pen, Digitising Pad, Digital Plotter

Many CAD systems use a **light pen** for input. This is a pen which will draw lines on the graphics screen of the computer. Lines can be drawn freehand, or straight line segments moved on the screen until they are in the right position. The advantage of a light pen is that it draws directly onto the screen. Its disadvantage is that it is somewhat difficult to position accurately. It is also tiring to hold a pen in the air for a long time.

A more precise method of drawing into a CAD system is to use a **digitising pad**. This consists of a flat white pad, sometimes marked with squares. A small indicator is moved across the pad. A point or

A Hewlett-Packard CAD system used for designing mechanical components. It uses a digitising pad for input.

cross appears on the computer screen at a position corresponding to that of the indicator. Some digitisers do not need a pad — they can be moved across the surface of a desk. A digitising pad is more precise than a light pen, but does not draw on the screen directly.

The display screen of a CAD system shows **graphics** as well as text. Lines can be positioned precisely, and various types of shading can be displayed. Text can be vertical or horizontal, and can be in different sizes. The positioning of text and graphics is much more precise than on an ordinary computer. Some CAD systems are in colour.

Printed output from a CAD system is made on a **digital plotter**. This moves one or more pens across a large sheet of paper under computer control. The pens draw lines of various widths. Some digital plotters have several colours. The pen is lowered to touch the surface of the paper to draw a line, or raised to move to another position. Text can be written onto a diagram. The letters can be a variety of sizes, and running in any direction. Plotting a complete plan can take some time: several minutes for one with many lines.

QUESTIONS

1 What advantage does a light pen have over a digitising pad? What advantage does a digitising pad have over a light pen?

2 Is a digital plotter faster or slower than other output devices?

3 In what way does the screen of a CAD system differ from that of an ordinary computer?

7.6 CAD in Practice

An IBM computer system being used for the design of logic circuits.

Computer-aided design is gradually becoming the standard way of doing all design work. Most firms of architects and engineers are installing CAD equipment. The design of cars, trucks, aircraft and spacecraft is done almost entirely on CAD systems.

In the electronics industry, microchips are designed with the aid of sophisticated computers. The CAD systems are used to produce the **artwork** from which the chips are made. They also test the designs. Most **printed circuit boards**, on which chips are mounted in computers, are designed with the aid of computers. These CAD systems can work out the shortest paths between the chips.

Computers are used increasingly in the making of films and television programmes. CAD systems can be used to draw cartoons, and to produce special effects. Images from the computer can be combined with film taken in the usual way. Lettering can be superimposed on a television image as it is being broadcast.

The main benefit of computer-aided design is its flexibility. Changes can be made quickly, and the effects of the changes on the whole design can be looked at. When a large number of people have a say in a design, this can save a lot of time!

CAD systems also eliminate much of the repetitive work in developing a design. Once an image has been entered, views of it from all angles can be displayed and printed. This saves the time taken to draw these views on paper. A large building needs thousands of drawings — many of these can be printed from a small number of basic designs on a CAD system.

The biggest problem facing firms which want to install CAD systems is cost. A CAD system costs tens of thousands of pounds per workstation. The total cost often runs into millions. Small firms cannot always afford these costs. An additional problem is staff attitudes and training. Many architects and engineers find it difficult to work with designs in three dimensions. Few have any training on CAD systems — they must be trained by their

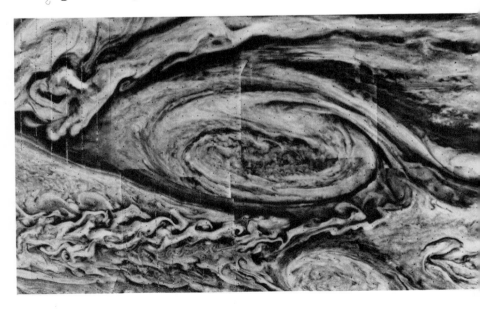

An image processing system being used to assemble a composite photograph of the Red Spot on the surface of Jupiter. The photographs were taken by the Voyager 1 satellite, and show details as small as 33 kilometres across.

companies. Accordingly, many firms are introducing computers for design work over a number of years. This spreads the cost, and makes training easier. However, they all realise that any company which falls behind in the move to CAD is unlikely to stay in business for long.

CAD enables companies to do more design work with fewer staff. This is leading to a reduction in the number of jobs, particularly for draughtsmen. This loss is offset by a greater emphasis on design, particularly in furniture, household goods, vehicles and advertising. These new opportunities for designers are creating jobs.

QUESTIONS

1 List the main advantages of computer-aided design.

2 What are the problems facing a company which wants to install a CAD system?

3 Why does CAD place small firms at a disadvantage?

4 What is likely to happen to design companies which do not install CAD systems in the near future?

5 What effects is CAD having on jobs?

A tesselation (see question 2 overleaf).

Exercise 7

1 Write down the meanings of the folliwng terms: plan, elevation, perspective view, computer-aided design, light pen, digitising pad, graphics, digital plotter.

2 **Tesselations** are shapes which fit into each other to form a continuous pattern. Squares and rectangles can be tesselated; so can many other shapes. Tesselations are used for floor tiles and fabric patterns.

Either use a special tesselations program, or the CAD program on your school's computer. Experiment with the effects you can produce with tesselated shapes.

a) Produce one or more designs for floor tiles. The shapes should be interesting but not too difficult to manufacture! Try various colour combinations with each design. Print the best ones.

b) Design some fabric patterns based on tesselations. Decide whether your fabric is for clothes or furniture, and base each design on a theme. Print the best designs.

3 Use the CAD program on your school's computer for some of the following exercises. Follow the same overall steps as in the activities in this chapter:

- A cartoon story, possibly as part of your class newspaper.
- A map — draw a basic outline and store it on disk. Then call the outline up and produce a series of maps showing different features: roads, rivers, land use, power lines, etc.
- The design for a bookshelf, chair or other item of furniture.
- A motorway junction.
- The street plan of a town.
- The design of a house. Produce a plan of each floor, and elevations of each wall. Try different designs for the windows and doors, and different types of roof. Also try out various colour schemes!
- The layout for a railway station, junction or section of track.

Things to Find Out

1 Find out if there are any companies near your school which use computer-aided design. The most likely are large firms of architects, engineering companies, design studios and possibly the town planning department of your local authority. Find out how the CAD systems are used, and what are their benefits and drawbacks.

2 Find out the cost of the kind of CAD system described in the story at the start of this chapter. Discuss how the system might justify this cost.

Points to Discuss

1 When a firm of architects introduces computer-aided design, the staff are trained in its use. Training courses are not usually very long, and afterwards the architects are expected to start using the CAD system in their work. Some architetcts find the training courses too short, and have great difficulties in using the CAD equipment.

Discuss the problems facing an architect who has ten years left before he retires, and is finding it almost impossible to adapt to the use of CAD.

2 The complicated circuits on a microchip could not be designed without a CAD system. The CAD systems used for microchip design are very expensive, and include features for checking the operation of the designs, before they are made.

a) Find out more about the use of CAD in the design of microchips.

b) Discuss the problems facing a new company which is set up to produce microchips, which arise from the cost of the CAD system.

3 Many of the problems found in buildings constructed in the last twenty years are due to bad design. Bad designs encourage vandalism, and make it easier for criminals to commit crimes, and to escape. The people who live in badly designed buildings are more likely to be ill, and to suffer from nervous problems.

a) Discuss other effects of bad design in buildings.

b) Discuss ways in which CAD can be used to ensure that the mistakes of the past are not repeated in new buildings.

4 Over the last few years, the design of furniture, household goods, toys and motor cars has improved a great deal.

a) Find some photographs of old and new items such as bicycles, toys, furniture etc.

b) Discuss the benefits of better design for the people who buy and use the goods, and for the people who make and sell them.

Viewdata

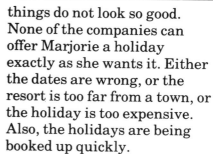

● Marjorie Hughes has decided to take her daughters to a Greek island for their summer holiday. She goes to a local travel agent. The travel agent has a number of brochures from companies which have holidays in Greece. Marjorie looks through them. They all look so inviting, she doesn't know which holiday to choose!

To help her make the choice, the travel agent writes down a list of all her requirements. She wants to be near a beach, but not too far from a town. She can only go during the first three weeks of August. The holiday must not cost more than a certain amount.

The travel agent then telephones the holiday companies. After several calls, things do not look so good. None of the companies can offer Marjorie a holiday exactly as she wants it. Either the dates are wrong, or the resort is too far from a town, or the holiday is too expensive. Also, the holidays are being booked up quickly.

Eventually Marjorie decides that there are two holidays to choose from. The travel agent telephones these companies again, and takes an option on both holidays for Marjorie. Marjorie goes home with the brochures to make her choice.

She discusses the two alternatives with her daughters, and together they decide on the one they prefer. Marjorie fills in the booking form.

The next day she returns to the travel agent with her form. The agent telephones the one holiday company to confirm the booking, and the other one to cancel Marjorie's option. Marjorie writes out a cheque for the deposit. The agent completes the form and gives Marjorie a receipt. Later she posts the form to the holiday company. A week later she receives a confirmation of the booking back through the post. She posts this to Marjorie.

● Winston Myatt has decided to take his family to the Caribbean for their holiday this year. He wants to watch some cricket while they are there. This means that there are only a few dates on which he can travel. He writes down a list of the things he wants for his holiday, and goes to see a travel agent.

The travel agent has a **viewdata** computer system on his desk. This is linked to a central computer by telephone. The computer has details of a number of holidays from different companies. The information about the holidays is displayed on the travel agent's screen.

Winston tells the travel agent what kind of holiday he wants, and shows him the list of dates and other details. The travel agent uses his viewdata system to call up information about possible holidays. He discusses them with Winston as they look at the screen.

Several holidays look promising, and the agent checks which dates these are available. Although none are exactly what Winston wants, they agree that one is much better than all the others. Winston decides to choose this holiday.

The travel agent enters Winston's name, address and dates of travel into the viewdata system. He also enters Winston's credit card number, so that the holiday can be paid for on his credit card. They check the information on the screen. The agent then confirms the booking, and the computer prints a slip giving details of the holiday.

Winston takes the slip home to his family. They are all excited that their holiday has already been booked.

QUESTIONS

1 How long did it take to book each holiday? Comment on your answers.

2 How many telephone calls did the first travel agent have to make to book the holiday? How many did the second travel agent make? Comment on your answers.

3 Would Marjorie Hughes have been able to finalise her booking if she had made up her mind in the travel agent's? How much extra work did her indecision cause?

8.1 A Viewdata System

A **viewdata** system has a central computer which stores a large amount of information arranged as **pages**. Each page is one screenful of information. The computer is linked to a number of **terminals**, by telephone lines. The terminals may be special viewdata terminals, or television sets with viewdata adaptors. Microcomputers can also be used as viewdata terminals. Figure 8.1 shows how the terminals are linked to the central computer.

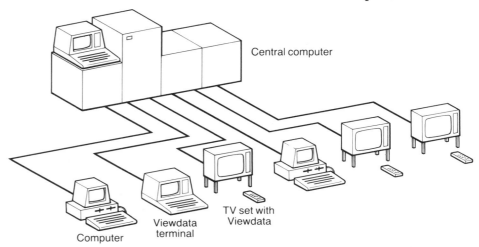

Figure 8.1: A viewdata network

When you use a viewdata system, you start by dialling the number of the central computer. When your terminal or microcomputer is connected, you first see a header page. You can then move to other pages by pressing keys on the terminal. Figure 8.2 shows how to move from one page to another. Each page has a number — if you know the number, you can go straight to the the page without having to work your way down from the header page.

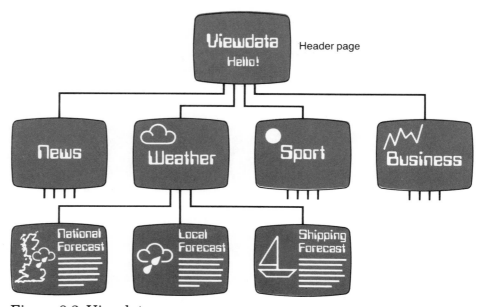

Figure 8.2: Viewdata pages

The largest viewdata system in Britain is the **Prestel** system run by British Telecom. It is based on a number of regional computers - you are linked automatically to the nearest one when you dial in. Prestel is used by a number of businesses, including travel agents, insurance companies and banks. It is also used by people with terminals at home. Among the things you can do on Prestel are:

- Look at the latest news, weather forecasts and sports results.

- Look at train, air and coach timetables, and book tickets.

- Book theatre tickets.

- Look at catalogues of goods, and enter orders for goods.

- Look at information about farming conditions and the prices of farm produce.

- Look at up-to-date financial information such as share prices and exchange rates of foreign currencies.

- Look at information about college courses, and send off for more details of these courses.

- Business users can book holidays and do other transactions — all from their Prestel terminals!

- Send messages to other Prestel users.

Many schools use Prestel. They use the Prestel Education pages to exchange information and find out about conferences and courses. Files of information for use with information retrieval programs and spreadsheets can be loaded onto the Prestel computers, and copied from them by schools. Schools make extensive use of the general Prestel pages for educational purposes.

Another Prestel service is **Micronet 800**, for home computer enthusiasts. Micronet enables users to see the latest news about home computers, computer games and other programs. It also enables users to swap programs.

There are a number of **local viewdata** systems in Britain, some of which link groups of schools. All work in more or less the same way as Prestel.

QUESTIONS

1 In what ways are home users most likely to use viewdata?

2 How is viewdata of use to farmers?

3 Which company runs the Prestel system?

4 What services are offered by Micronet 800?

● **ACTIVITY**

8.2 Plan a Holiday

In this section, you will use Prestel or a local viewdata system to plan a holiday. You will stay at a hotel for a week, and travel by train, coach or air from your home town to the holiday hotel.

Before you use the computer, decide which town you would like to visit, how many people there will be in your party, and when you would like to travel. Decide how much money you can spend on the holiday. Write these things down.

Run the program which links your school's computer to Prestel or a local viewdata service. Telephone the central computer, and link your computer to it. Follow the instructions for Prestel or the local viewdata system.

● Find the pages with details of hotels. Look to see which ones have rooms available when you want to travel. Also look at the rates for the rooms.

● When you have chosen a suitable hotel, write down the details: name, address, dates and the cost of the stay. (If you are using Prestel, do not actually make a booking!)

● Then look at the rail, air and coach timetables. Decide how you are going to travel to the hotel from your home town. Write down the times and other details of the trains, coaches and air flights you will catch. (Once again, do not actually make any bookings!)

● Look up the fares for these journeys. Write them down and calculate the total cost of travel. (If they are not on the viewdata system, try to find them out from a newspaper or by some other means. Otherwise estimate them.)

● Decide how much money you are going to take to spend. If you are travelling to a foreign country, look up the conversion rates for that country. Work out how much local currency you will get.

● Away from the computer, write a report giving all the details of your holiday. Calculate the total cost. Can you do it on the amount of money you originally allowed?

QUESTIONS

1 In what other ways could you have planned this holiday? Did the viewdata system make it easier to plan all the details?

2 How long did it take to plan the holiday? During this time, your computer is linked via a telephone line to the central computer. Find out the price of telephone calls, and work out the cost of this call. Also find out the costs of using the viewdata service, if there are any. Comment on these costs.

3 If you had to change your travel plans at the last minute, for example because a train or air flight was cancelled, how easily do think you could book an alternative? Comment on the benefits of a viewdata system for these purposes.

95

8.3 School Viewdata — News and Weather

In this activity, you will set up a small viewdata system on your school's computer. It will contain news and weather reports, specially adapted for your area. This activity may be done by a group of pupils, and can form the basis of an extended project.

Before you use the computer, look again at Figure 8.2, which shows how the pages of a viewdata system are linked. The pages are in a 'tree' structure, with the header page at the top. From any page, you can press a key to select one of the pages 'below' it in the tree. You can also return to the page 'above' it.

Plan the structure of the pages for your local viewdata system in a similar way. Decide which keys will have to be pressed to choose other pages in the tree.

Decide which pages you will copy from Prestel or another viewdata system, and which you will enter yourself. Once you have copied the pages into your own system, you may edit them. For example, you may change the instructions for choosing other pages from the page you are on.

Plan the new pages carefully. Use large text for headings, and choose suitable colours. Too many colours makes a viewdata page look confusing! Do not put too much text into a page – pay careful attention to the wording which you use.

- Link your school's computer to Prestel or your local viewdata service. Choose the pages of news and weather which you want for your own viewdata system, and copy them into your 'jotter'. Look at the instructions for the viewdata program on your computer for the method of doing this.

- Close down the link to Prestel or the local viewdata service. Open up a new set of viewdata pages on your computer.

- Copy the pages from your 'jotter' into their places in the set. Edit them so that they are properly linked to the pages above and below them in the structure.

- Enter the new pages which contain local news and weather. Use a local newspaper for this information. Do not copy the news – write it in short sentences so that it fits neatly into the viewdata pages.

- Choose a title for your viewdata service, and design a title page. Make it as attractive as possible!

- When all the pages are complete, look through them all, checking that they are linked properly.

- Make sure that your set of pages is properly stored on disk before you close down the computer.

QUESTIONS

1 Make a list of the possible uses for your viewdata news and weather service, both in your school and elsewhere. For example, it might be used in local community centres or hospitals if the equipment were available. Comment on these uses.

2 What are the benefits of a local viewdata news system for a handicapped person with limited use of their hands?

● **ACTIVITY**   8.4 **Portfolio Manager**

The trading floor of the London Stock Exchange. This is due to be closed down when the electronic share dealing systems are fully in use.

All businesses need money in order to start trading. This money, the **capital**, is used to buy offices, factories and equipment. It is used for initial supplies of raw materials, and for the costs of developing products, before they can be sold. Many companies raise this capital by selling **shares** in the business.

When you buy a share in a company, you are supplying part of the capital it needs. If the company makes a profit, some of the profit is divided among the shareholders. These **dividends** are paid once or twice a year.

The shares in companies are not always kept by their original investors. They are bought and sold on **stock exchanges**, such as the one in London. The prices of the shares go up and down all the time. If a company is expected to do well, the price of its shares goes up. If its prospects are bad, its share price can drop very quickly. Share

97

```
CET Local Viewdata System          312b
NAME Computer Education        10-OCT-85


              Base    Price   Value  % Ch


U-Acorn Cmpt  077-00  73-00     365   5.1
Allied`Lyons  276-00  280-00   1400   1.4
Beattie(J) A  083-00  78-00     390   6.0
Manders       196-00  184-00    920   6.1
U-Northamber  183-00  163-00    815  10.9
U-Owners Abr  025-00  24-04     121   2.9
Pilkton.Bros  265-00  258-00   1290   2.6
Superdrug     436-00  438-00   2190   0.4
Tarmac        340-00  346-00   1730   1.7
Wolver Dud.   390-00  378-00   1890   3.0

  1 View Portfolio     2 Summary
  3 Select Portfolio   4 New Portfolio
  5 Add   6 Delete      7 Amend an Entry
                        9 CitiService
```

prices are also affected by the state of the economy, inflation rates, oil prices, etc. No one can predict for sure what is going to happen to them next!

The aim of this activity is to 'buy' a **portfolio** of shares, and then see how the prices of the shares change over a period of time. Changes in the total value of the portfolio can be worked out. This activity is most suitable for older pupils who have some background knowledge of shares, inflation and the economy in general.

Before using the computer, allocate yourself a sum of money to invest (say £1000). Think about the types of shares you wish to invest in. Some large companies such as British Telecom or Sainsbury have prospects of steady growth. Smaller, newer companies such as Amstrad may grow more quickly, but have a higher risk. Most portfolios contain a mixture of the two types of share.

- Call up the share price pages on Prestel or your local viewdata system, and look at them carefully. Look at the changes in the prices since the previous day. Think about the prospects of each company over the next few weeks.

- Decide which companies you want to invest in. Select up to six companies, and allocate yourself a suitable number of shares in each, so that you 'spend' the sum of money you have to invest.

- Draw up a table as set out below to record your portfolio. If possible, enter the table into a spreadsheet.

Company	Number of shares	Price 17/07/86	Value 17/07/86	Price 24/07/86	Value 24/07/86
Amstrad	100	£1.16	£116.00		
Br T'com	100	£2.00	£200.00		
Plessey	100	£2.18	£218.00		
Granada	100	£2.80	£280.00		
Wedgwood	60	£3.23	£193.80		
Total			£1007.80		

- One week later, look up the prices of the shares in your portfolio again. Enter the prices in the table, and work out the values of the shares. Also work out the total value of the portfolio.

- Continue this process for several weeks.

- Plot a graph showing, on the same axes, the prices of the shares in your portfolio and the total value of the portfolio, over the weeks.

- Look at the way in which the prices of the shares have changed. Try to explain these changes — take into account the state of the economy, any changes in government policy, changes in oil prices or interest rates, and any other factors which might be relevant (even the weather!).

8.5 Computer Elements: Modem, Fibre Optics Links, Microwave and Satellite Links

In order to connect a computer to a telephone line, a special device called a **modem** is used. It changes the signals from the ways they are represented inside the computer to the way they are sent along a telephone line. The modem at the other end of the telephone line changes the signals back again (see Figure 8.3). Some modems have additional facilities such as the ability to dial the number of the other computer automatically.

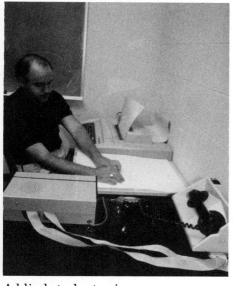

A blind student using a computer terminal which produces Braille output. On the right is a modem which connects the terminal via the telephone line to a computer.

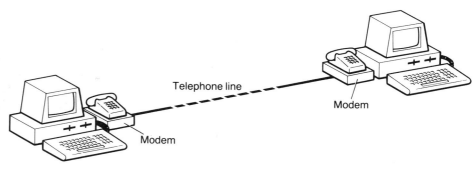

Figure 8.3: Computers connected via modems and telephone line

Until a few years ago, all telephone lines were made of metal, in most cases copper. Now **fibre optics** cable is being used instead. Fibre optics cable consists of a number of very thin strands of pure glass. Signals are sent as pulses of light along these strands. Fibre optics cables can carry far more telephone calls than copper cables. They also give much clearer signals, and are cheaper than copper cables.

Many of the **trunk lines** which carry all the telephone calls between large cities use **microwave radio** links. These use special dishes on towers such as the Telecom Tower in London which are pointing directly at each other. The radio signals are sent from one dish to another (see Figure 8.4). Microwave links can carry large numbers of calls, and are cheap, as no cables are involved.

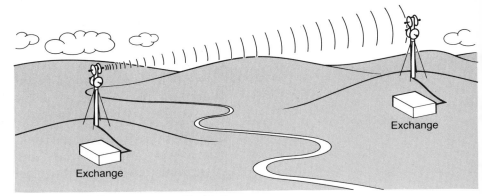

Figure 8.4: Microwave radio link

International telephone calls and long-distance messages between computers are often sent via **communications satellites**. These are in orbits which make them appear to be stationary above a point on the earth's equator. Most of them are over the middle of oceans. Signals are sent up to the satellite from one side of the ocean, and sent down from the satellite to the other side (see Figure 8.5). The satellites can handle more calls than cables laid on the seabed from one continent to another.

A communications satellite — the small dishes send and receive the signals, the large panels collect solar energy to power the satellite.

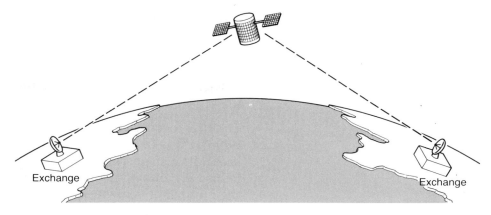

Figure 8.5: Satellite communications link

Viewdata systems are only one of a number of computer services which combine computing with communications systems. The ability to process information on a computer, and then send it rapidly to where it is needed, is one of the major benefits of information technology.

QUESTIONS

1. Why is a modem necessary when connecting a computer to a telephone line? What additional functions do some modems perform?

2. List **four** ways in which a telephone signal can be carried.

3. What are the advantages of fibre optics cables over copper cables?

4. What is the advantage of microwave radio over other ways of construction telephone trunk lines?

5. Why are computers and communications systems such a powerful combination?

8.6 Viewdata in Practice

Prestel is the main viewdata service in Britain. It is run by British Telecom on behalf of a large number of **information providers**. These supply the pages of information, and the services associated with the information. Subscibers pay a fee to join Prestel, and a charge for the time they spend using it. Some pages cost an additional fee for viewing.

Many of the information providers have **response frames**, which are 'forms' that can be filled in on the screen. These are used to order goods, request more information, make bank transactions, or even to place bets on horses! Response frames are also used to send messages to other users.

At present, Prestel has eight main topics: banking, travel, insurance, shopping, business, agriculture, microcomputing and education. All users can see information on all of these topics. Some users, such as travel agents, can see additional pages, not accessible to ordinary users. These pages include **gateways** to other computers, for example computers belonging to holiday companies. By means of these gateways, holiday bookings can be made.

The Prestel service has been in operation for a number of years. When it was first introduced, it was somewhat slow in attracting users. Its concentration on a small number of specific areas has helped it gain popularity. The number of information providers and the number of users are growing steadily.

QUESTIONS

1 What **eight** topics does the Prestel service cover at present?

2 Was Prestel very popular when it was first introduced? What has helped it to gain in popularity?

3 Can all Prestel users see the same information?

4 How does a user order goods on Prestel?

Exercise 8

1 Write down the meanings of the following words or phrases: viewdata, page, terminal, local viewdata service, portfolio, modem, fibre optics, trunk line, information provider, response frame, gateway.

2 Enter a set of viewdata pages on your school's computer for some of the following purposes:

a) To prepare an information base of local amenities and events - see Exercise 2, Question 4. Enter pages for the films at local cinemas, the plays at local theatres, sporting events, etc. Design each page as attractively as possible, and include simple pictures. Include pages from Prestel or your local viewdata system if any are suitable.

This activity can be done by a group of pupils, sharing the work of research and entering pages. When all the pages have been entered, check the set carefully to ensure that they are linked together properly.

This set of pages can be kept up-to-date by other groups of pupils once it has been entered. It can form the basis of an extended project.

b) If your school is having an Open Day or Parents' Evening, set up a viewdata system for a computer in the school foyer. This carries information on the various activities, and where each activity is to be found. Try to enter a simple map of the school on one of the pages.

c) Set up a viewdata system giving information about the optional subjects which may be chosen by pupils starting their Fourth year. Include brief details of each subject, and the examinations to which it leads. (A similar set of viewdata pages could be set up for Sixth Form subjects.)

d) Set up a viewdata system giving details of local job opportunities. Get the information from the school careers office, local Job Centre or local newspapers. Include any pages from your local viewdata system which are suitable. For each job, include the qualifications required, the location, working hours, starting salary and brief details of the work. Plan the structure of the set of pages carefully, so that similar jobs are grouped under header pages.

3 Follow the steps of the activity in Section 8.2 to plan a school journey by coach or train to a place of interest in a town some distance away. Calculate the total cost of the journey, and the cost per pupil going on the journey.

4 Copy a sequence of pages of Prestel weather reports from successive days into a 'jotter'. Then assemble these pages into a viewdata sequence. Scan through the pages and write a summary of the trends in the weather during the period you have recorded.

Things to Find Out

1 Viewdata systems like Prestel are stored on central computers, which are linked to users by telephone. **Teletext** systems contain a small number of pages of information, sent out as television signals. They can be viewed on television sets which have teletext facilities. In Britain, the viewdata systems are called **Ceefax** and **Oracle**.
a) Find out more about Ceefax and Oracle: what kinds of information they carry, how they are used, how much they cost to use, etc.
b) List some similarities and some differences between viewdata systems and teletext systems.

2 The Bank of Scotland provides a home banking service on Prestel. The Nottingham Building Society provides a similar service. Find out more about these services. Write a report on them, giving details of the facilities provided, and the advantages of using viewdata for these purposes.

3 Services similar to viewdata in other European contries include: **Minitel** in France; **Viditel** in Holland; **Bildschirntext** in West Germany.
Choose **one** of these services and find out in what ways it is similar to Prestel, and in what ways it differs. Write a report on your findings.

4 Find out which local businesses use Prestel, and for what purposes. Find out what benefits they have derived from Prestel.

Points to Discuss

1 Discuss the advantages and disadvantages of ordering goods from shops via Prestel.

2 Using the information from Question 1 in the previous section, discuss the benefits of home banking services via viewdata.

3 Each Prestel user has a **mailbox** which contains the messages sent to him or her by other users. Some time ago, someone managed to 'break into' the mailbox belonging to the Duke of Edinburgh, read the messages in it, and insert another message.
a) Discuss the consequences of someone breaking into your Prestel mailbox. What measures would you take to prevent this?
b) Discuss the general issue of security of information on a viewdata system.

4 A number of additional Prestel facilities are becoming available. It is now possible to search pages of information for key words, and to set up a sequence of pages which can be called up and viewed by pressing a single key. In the near future it will be possible to link Prestel to other software. High-resolution graphics Prestel pages are also a possibility. A new application which is already beginning is the use of Prestel to transfer data files between other programs. For example, spreadsheets can be stored on the Prestel computers, and loaded by Prestel users onto their computers.

a) Find out more about these new Prestel facilities.
b) Discuss the benefits they might bring.
c) Suggest some additional facilities for Prestel or local viewdata services.
d) At present Prestel is used only by a small number of households in Britain. Discuss the likely growth in the number of home users, as more facilities become available. This discussion might take the form of a debate between those who think that all homes will eventually be linked to Prestel, and those who do not.

CHAPTER 9

Electronic mail

● Peter Williams is feeling very pleased with himself. His company, Reforge Valves, has just reached agreement to supply a set of valves to a shipping company, ABK Lines, in Singapore. The valves are worth more than one million pounds. He has to draw up the contract for the sale, and send it to Singapore for the first payment to be made.

He makes a rough draft of the contract. Most of it consists of standard paragraphs which are the same on all Reforge contracts. A few of these have slight changes, and there are some additional paragraphs which he writes out by hand.

He gives his notes to his secretary, Beverley Cole. She types a **draft** of the contract, copying the standard paragraphs from a form, and typing Peter's ones as best she can. She brings the draft to Peter, who reads it very carefully. He marks all the errors, and makes a few changes.

Beverley then types the **top copy** of the contract. She types very slowly, because each time she makes a mistake, she has to re-type the whole page. After an hour, she has finished. Peter then checks the contract again, and gives Beverley a page to retype.

Finally he is satisfied, and signs it.

Beverley takes the contract to the Post Office, and sends it by registered post. Five days later, it arrives in Singapore.

Lee Yuan, the supplies manager of ABK Lines, reads the contract carefully. He telephones his company's bank, and asks them to make out a **banker's draft** for the first payment to Reforge Valves. Later in the day, the bank sends a messenger with the draft. Lee Yuan signs it, and sends it by registered post to Reforge Valves. It arrives six days later.

Peter Williams checks the banker's draft, and asks Beverley Cole to take it to the bank. He then goes to see the production manager, and asks him to begin work on the valves.

• Joanna Ferguson puts down the telephone. She has just reached an agreement for her company, Plexus Electronics, to supply a set of cash terminals to the Hong Kong International Bank. The order is worth several million pounds.

Joanna has a cup of tea while she thinks about the contract for the sale. She starts up the word processing program on her desktop computer. She opens up a new document for the contract, and copies a set of standard paragraphs into it. She amends two of these paragraphs, and adds three more which are particular to this sale.

Joanna checks the whole contract very carefully, and prints a **draft** of it. She takes it to her divisional manager, Jonathan Bellwood, who checks it with her, and initials it. Joanna makes the final corrections back at her desk, and saves the contract on disk.

She then calls up the **electronic mail** program on her computer. She sends the contract directly from her computer to the **mailbox** of the Hong Kong International Bank. Joanna telephones Teng Kwon Hua at the bank in Hong Kong to tell him that the contract has been sent. Teng Kwon Hua is about to go home — it is late in the evening in Hong Kong!

The next morning, Teng Kwon Hua runs the electronic mail program on his desktop computer. He checks his mailbox and finds that the

contract from Plexus Electronics is there. He copies it to his computer, and saves it on disk. He then looks at it, using his word processing system. When he he has read it carefully, he calls the accounts department to authorise the first payment.

The accountant calls one of the cashiers and asks her to make an **electronic funds transfer** to Plexus Electronics. She enters the details of the transfer at her terminal. The money is deducted from the Hong Kong International Bank's own account and a message is sent to the computer at Lloyds Bank in Britain, transferring the money into the account of Plexus Electronics.

When Joanna gets to work the same morning (by which time it is afternoon in Hong Kong), she calls Lloyds Bank

to confirm that the money has been transferred. She then goes to see Jonathan Bellwood, who authorises the production department to start work on the cash terminals for the Hong Kong International Bank.

QUESTIONS

1 How long did it take for the first payment for the contract to reach Peter Williams? How long did the payment take to reach Joanna Ferguson? Comment on the difference in these times.

2 How was the payment for the contract transferred in each case?

3 What difficulty is there in doing business by telephone between the UK and the Far East?

9.1 Electronic Mail and Electronic Funds Transfer

Electronic mail is a method of sending messages between computers. Each user on the network has a **mailbox** which holds incoming messages. Outgoing messages are sent to the mailboxes of users to whom they are addressed. Users can copy messages from their mailboxes into their own computers whenever they want to. There are central **message switching** computers which direct the messages from the sender to the receiver's mailbox (see Figure 9.1).

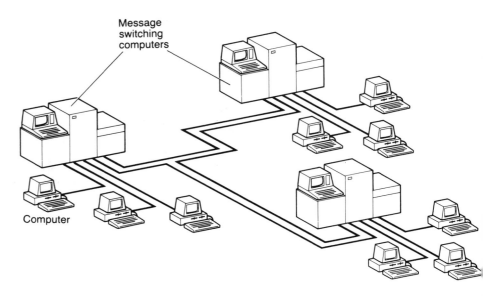

Figure 9.1: Electronic mail network

Many types of messages can be sent. The majority are word processor documents. These are typed and edited in the usual way, and stored on disk. They are then sent from the disk by the electronic mail program. The person receiving the message copies it from his or her mailbox onto a word processing data disk. The document can then be viewed on the screen and printed as required. Other types of messages include invoices, booking forms, and records from databases.

Electronic funds transfer (EFT) is a special type of message service between banks. When a sum of money is to be transferred from one bank account to another, the sending bank enters a withdrawal on its computer. It sends a message to the computer of the receiving bank. The message travels via the EFT network, which links major banks throughout the world. The receiving bank transfers the sum of money into the receiving account. The transaction takes only a few seconds, and no paperwork is generated.

Another type of message service has a large central store of information which is accessed by users. There are a variety of these systems, covering such topics as legal cases, chemicals and summaries of scientific papers. Users call up the central computer

Computers in use for electronic funds transfer at a bank in New York.

and look at the information on their computer screens. They copy the records they want to their computers.

The **message switching computers** work like telephone exchanges in the electronic mail network. They route incoming messages to their destinations. They automatically choose the best path for the message, and can try an alternative path if one is not working. They have the mailboxes for all their local users. They also have temporary storage for messages in transit. This means that computers of different types can be connected together in the network — they do not all have to send and receive messages at the same speed.

Connections between message switching computers can be made by copper or fibre optics cables, microwave radio links or even via communications satellites (see Chapter 8 for details).

There are several electronic mail systems in Britain. The largest is the **Telecom Gold** service operated by British Telecom. Many schools are linked by **The Times Network for Schools (TTNS)**. The **Swift** network, based in Belgium, handles electronic funds transfers between banks all over the world.

QUESTIONS

1 List the steps when a document is sent by electronic mail from one computer user to another.

2 What types of messages are sent by electronic mail? Include those mentioned in the text and any others you know of.

3 What tasks are performed by message switching computers?

4 How long does it take to transfer a sum of money by EFT?

9.2 Send a Letter to a Pen Friend

In this activity you will prepare a letter to a pen friend on your word processor. You will then send it via electronic mail. Your pen friend will be at another school — possibly in another country.

Before you use the computer, decide what to include in your letter. You might want to tell your pen friend about yourself, your family, your town or your school, or something about all of these. Decide whether you are going to describe your hobbies, your pets or your favourite pop groups. Make some notes to help you plan your letter.

- Use the word processing system on your school's computer to type and check your letter, and store it on disk. Follow the instructions in Section 2.2.

- Make a note of the reference of the letter on disk. You will need this reference when using the electronic mail program.

  Find out the **mailbox number** of the pen friend to whom you are going to send the letter.

- Run the electronic mail program on your school's computer and connect it to the telephone. Follow the instructions for the program to find out how to carry out each operation.

- Send the letter to your pen friend's mailbox. Enter the reference of the letter and your pen friend's mailbox number when you are asked to do so.

- Look in your own mailbox to see if there are any letters waiting for you. If so, copy them onto the disk which contains your word processing documents.

- Close down the electronic mail program. Use your word processing program to look at the letters you have received.

QUESTIONS

1 How long did it take you to write your letter on the word processor, and send it via electronic mail? Compare this with the time it would have taken for the letter to have been written by hand and posted. Comment on the difference in times.

2 Find out the cost of sending a letter by electronic mail. Compare this cost with the postage cost for a printed version of the same letter. Comment on the differences in cost.

9.3 Foreign Correspondent

Most newspapers have reporters in foreign countries. These **foreign correspondents** follow events in the country in which they are stationed, and send reports back to their newspapers. It is important to get these reports back as quickly as possible. They must arrive before the reports from the foreign correspondents of competing

High-speed communications in days gone by: a messenger landing from a boat near Dover, and passing a dispatch from a foreign correspondent of 'The Times' to a rider bound for London.

newspapers! In the past, these reports were sent by dispatch riders on horseback, by boat, carrier pigeon or hot air balloon. Today they are sent by telephone or electronic mail.

The job of foreign correspondent has always been difficult, exciting and sometimes dangerous. Foreign correspondents must cover wars, rebellions, strikes and overthrows of governments as well as sports matches and cultural events. Many countries have restrictions on what can be reported about events which happen in them.

If your class has a class newspaper (Activity 2.4), appoint some of your pen friends as foreign correspondents. If any of your pen friends have class newspapers, even if they are not produced on a word processor, ask to become a foreign correspondent for their newspaper. You may have to send your reports in a foreign language — this is a small problem for a good foreign correspondent!

The job of the foreign correspondent is as follows:

- Look out for events which are going to be worth reporting. Think about the kind of events which would interest the readers of the newspaper in the other country. They will want to know all about the Royal Family, but a local football match might not interest them. On the other hand, they might find a local fashion show very interesting.

- If possible, go to the event you wish to cover yourself. Take along your reporter's notebook, and make notes of what you see. Ask people questions, but do not always believe their answers! Try to get at least two opinions on every topic.

- If you cannot cover an event yourself, watch reports of it on television, and listen to news about it on the radio. Get as many independent sources of information as you can. Make notes as you watch and listen.

- Draw up an outline of the report before you start typing it. Decide what main points you wish to make, and in what order.

- Use the word processing program on your school's computer to enter your report. See Sections 2.3 and 2.4 Check it very carefully and save it on disk.

- Call up the electronic mail program, and send it to the mailbox of your newspaper.

If you are receiving news from a foreign correspondent:

- Call up the electronic mail program, and check your mailbox, to see if any reports have arrived.

- Copy the reports to a disk containing the documents for your class newspaper.

- Close down the electronic mail program, and use the word processing program to edit the reports in the usual way (see Section 2.4).

QUESTIONS

1 In what ways are the jobs of local reporter and foreign correspondent different?

2 What difficulties does a foreign correspondent face in obtaining stories and getting them back to his or her newspaper?

3 What are the benefits of using electronic mail for sending reports by foreign correspondents?

● **ACTIVITY**

9.4 Sports League Matches

If your school and a number of neighbouring schools are on the same electronic mail newtork, it is an ideal way of arranging sports matches between them. Using electronic mail to arrange sports matches can form the basis of an extended project.

Most sports matches are organised in **leagues**. All the schools in the league take turns to play against each other. If possible, each school plays each other school twice, so that they each have a home and an away match.

One way of setting out the arrangements for a league is by means of a table, as shown below. It shows the matches between four schools.

| | | Away | | | |
		Highford	St Giles	Dean Row	The Vale
Home	Highford	—	4th May		
	St Giles		—		
	Dean Row			—	
	The Vale			4th May	—

The names of the schools are set out along the top and down the side fo the table. The side teams are the home teams; the top teams are the away teams. The dates are of the matches are filled into the table. In the above table, on 4th May, Highford is at home to St Giles and Dean Row travels to play The Vale.

Find out the dates for some sporting fixtures between your school, and neighbouring schools. If possible, help to arrange these dates.

- Set up a table, similar to the one shown above, with the names of the schools and the dates of the fixtures. Either use a spreadsheet program (Section 4.3), or a word processor (Section 2.2).

- Use the electronic mail program to send a copy of the table to all the other schools in the league. Include a note to them to check whether the dates for the fixtures are acceptable.

- If any of the dates need to be changed, amend the table, and send revised versions to the schools.

- As the matches are played, the dates in the table can be replaced by the results. Keep your copy of the table up-to-date with these results, and send copies of it to the other schools so that they all know the results.

- At the end of the season, send a final copy of the table, showing all the results, to all the schools in the league. (An alternative way of setting out the results for the league is to use a spreadsheet as described in Section 4.3.)

QUESTIONS

1 What are the benefits of arranging sports leagues in this way?

2 How easy is it to cope with changes in the dates of the fixtures, compared with the previous method of arranging them?

9.5 Computer Elements: Message Switching Computers

At the centre of an electronic mail or electronic funds transfer network are one or more **message switching computers**. These receive incoming messages, store them if necessary, and send them on to their destinations. They have the mailboxes for all the local users of the network.

A message switching computer is a mainframe or large minicomputer with some special hardware attached to it. The main items are a number of **multiplexers** which link the computer with the communications channels which make up the network. These enable a large number of channels to be connected to a small number of input and output ports in the computer. They also change the signals from the type used in the communications channels to those used by the computer.

A message switching computer in operation.

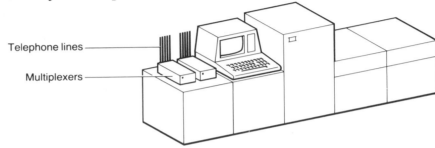

Figure 9.2: A message switching computer

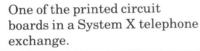

One of the printed circuit boards in a System X telephone exchange.

The message switching computer is controlled by special software which can receive the stream of messages, and decide very quickly where each one is to be sent. It also checks that all the messages which the computer sends are acknowledged by the computers which are to receive them. If a message is not acknowledged, it is sent again.

Very similar to message switching computers are the new **digital telephone exchanges** which are replacing the mechanical exchanges in Britain and most other industrial countries. These use specially designed hardware and software. They can accept telephone calls in digital form, as well as messages sent between computers. The commonest type of digital telephone exchange in the UK is the **System X** exchange made by Plessey for British Telecom.

QUESTIONS

1 What is the task of a multiplexer?

2 How does a message switching computer check that messages are being received?

3 What **two** types of message can a digital telephone exchange accept?

9.6 Electronic Mail in Practice

At present the main users of electronic message services are banks, insurance companies and other financial institutions. Most transactions between these companies are sent by electronic messages between their computers. The volume of messages of this sort is growing rapidly.

An increasing number of companies are using electronic mail for letters and contracts. Many of them send orders to suppliers and invoices customers via electronic mail. Researchers at universities and industrial laboratories use electronic mail to exchange experimental results and research papers.

'Time' magazine and other international publications have worldwide communications networks. These link their editorial offices and printing plants, which are located in key cities throughout the world. Reports are sent to the offices for the editions of the magazine to be prepared. The pages of the magazine are then sent as electronic messages to the printing plants. These are in countries closest to the largest numbers of readers of the magazine.

The underwriting room at the new headquarters of Lloyd's Insurance. The desks are equipped with electronic communications equipment.

A small number of home computer users are also linked to electronic mail networks, particularly in the USA. These enable them to send letters to each other, as well as files of information for spreadsheets, database programs and other software items. Chess matches are regularly played over electronic mail.

The benefits of electronic mail are its direct links with the computer systems of the senders and receivers, its high speed and low cost. The initial cost of equipment can be high, but once it is installed, the costs per message are low — much lower than sending the messages by any other means. Electronic mail is a relatively new service. It is likely to be one of the biggest growth areas in information technology over the next few years.

QUESTIONS

1 What types of company are the biggest users of electronic message services?

2 What are the main reasons for the rapid growth of electronic mail?

3 How do some home computer users make use of electronic mail?

Exercise 9

1 Write down the meanings of the following terms: banker's draft, electronic mail, mailbox, electronic funds transfer, message switching computer, foreign correspondent, multiplexer, digital telephone exchange.

2 Any of the following activities can be carried out if two or more schools on the same electronic mail network are willing to participate. The more schools that are involved, the better!

The majority of these activities are best carried out by groups of pupils over a period of time. The final result is a combined report, with tables, graphs, drawings and written descriptions.

In each case, sets of information are prepared using a word processor, spreadsheet or information retrieval package. These sets are then sent by electronic mail to other schools in the group. The information is examined by using the same software package as the one on which it was created.

a) Carry out a survey of local weather over a period of time, as described in Section 6.3. Exchange the results by electronic mail with other schools. Draw up combined tables and graphs which show as clearly as possible the contrasts between the weather recorded at the different places.

b) Carry out a survey of local items of historical interest – see Exercise 3 Question 5. Design a suitable record on an information retrieval system, and enter the results into it. Exchange the results by electronic mail with other schools — make sure that you are all using the same arrangement of records.

Collect the records from all the schools together, and look for similarities and differences. Make a combined display of the results, with pictures, tables and written descriptions.

c) Carry out a survey of local businesses or industries. For each company surveyed, decide what information to record. This might include:

Company name
Nature of business
Number of employees
Areas where products sold
Raw materials used
Where raw materials come from

Set up a file on an information retrieval program, using suitably designed records, for this information. Exchange this file via electronic mail for similar files created by other schools.

Look at the files from all the schools in the group. Try to identify patterns in the locations of different types of businesses. Write a report of your findings, including maps and diagrams.

d) The information from the wildlife survey (Section 3.4) can be exchanged between a number of schools which have carried out the survey. Reports can be written on the observations of animals and birds throughout the areas surveyed.

e) If there are chess enthusiasts at several schools on an electronic mail network, chess matches can be arranged over the network. Each player sends his or her next move as a message by electronic mail. Matches can be played over a few weeks, or during a special tournament, with moves entered directly into the electronic mail program.

Things to Find Out

1 Find out which local companies use electronic mail or other electronic message services. For those which do, find out how the systems work, and what the benefits are from using them.

2 The **telex** system is a forerunner of electronic mail. Most large companies have telex machines. It is now evolving into the **teletex** system. Find out more about the telex and teletex systems, and the similarities and differences between them and electronic mail.

3 The ultimate aim of telecommunications is to combine telephone, electronic mail, EFT, viewdata, cable television and a number of other message services into a single **integrated services digital network**. Find out more about the plans for an integrated services digital network. Discuss the benefits of a system of this nature, and any problems which might arise.

Points to Discuss

1 Electronic mail and electronic funds transfer are replacing the post and other delivery services by electronic systems based on the telecommunications network. Some people have predicted that the postal services will eventually close down. (In spite of these predictions, the volume of mail sent in the UK is increasing steadily.)

Discuss the consequences of electronic mail and EFT for the postal system.

2 Electronic mail allows users to send mesages from one computer to another. Viewdata allows users to look at large quantities of information on a central database. Both involve links between computers via telephone lines.

Although viewdata and electronic mail are different services, they have an increasing number of features in common. For example, some viewdata systems have mailboxes which allow users to exchange messages. Users of some electronic mail services can look at viewdata pages. Both viewdata and electronic mail services have gateways to other database systems.

a) Find out more about the common facilities provided by electronic mail and viewdata services.
b) Discuss the benefits which would arise if electronic mail and viewdata systems could be linked into a single system.

3 It is likely that advanced communications systems such as electronic mail and EFT will be of great benefit to the countries which install them. At present it is mainly industrial countries in Western Europe, North America and the Far East which can afford to set up systems of this nature. Many countries in Africa and South America are unlikely to install advanced telecommunications systems for a long time.

Discuss the consequences of this in widening the gap between rich and poor countries.

Control systems

● Roger Dawson's eyes are getting sore. He looks at the clock on the wall, and realises that there are still three hours left of his shift. A glance at his work schedule tells him that he still has seven sets of garment pieces to cut out.

He waits while the machine unrolls a length of cloth and folds it across the bed of his cutter to make forty layers. His assistant picks up the set of patterns for the pieces to be cut, and starts laying them out on top of the fabric. At first he cannot get them all to fit, but after several attempts he manages to arrange them.

Roger checks the list of pieces, to be sure that all those which should be in line with the run of the fabric are correctly aligned. One piece is not — he turns it around, and moves two other pieces to make room. Finally he is ready to start cutting.

Roger starts his knife cutter, and carefully guides it along the edge of the first piece. He works very slowly, and pauses from time to time to rub his eyes. A single slip could ruin all forty layers of cloth. After half an hour, he is finished. He realises that he is going to have to do the next six batches more quickly to finish his shift on time.

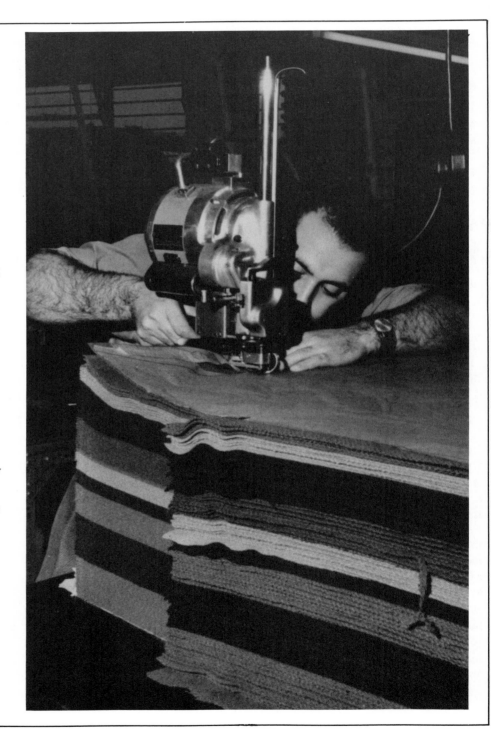

● Dougal MacFarlane looks up from the screen of his computer. He presses a key to start the next cutting cycle, and watches as the cutting machine automatically folds fifty layers of cloth onto the cutter bed.

On the screen appears a blank rectangle, and next to it are displayed the images of the cloth pieces which must fit into the rectangle. Those which can be rotated to fit are displayed in a different colour from the rest.

Dougal uses his light pen to move each pattern into a suitable place in the rectangle. He starts with the ones which cannot be rotated, and fills in the others later. It takes a few attempts to get them all in, but eventually he is satisfied. He presses a key, and the computer checks the arrangement. It highlights one place where two pieces are too close. Dougal adjusts the positions of these pieces. This time the computer is satisfied.

Dougal presses another key to start the cutting. The computer controls a laser cutter which moves along the edges of the pieces as shown on his screen. It cuts out the small pieces first, so that the weight of the cloth keeps everything in place. A point of light on the screen shows the position of the cutter — Dougal checks that it is working properly.

After a few minutes, the cutting is complete. Dougal gets up to help take the pieces off the cutting bed — it gives him a little exercise. He returns to his seat and starts up another cutting cycle.

QUESTIONS

1 How many layers of cloth could Roger cut in one hour? Assuming that a cutting cycle took Dougal fifteen minutes, how many could he cut in the same time? Comment on the differences between these times.

2 Roger's eyes were sore from watching his cutter and guiding it by hand. Could Dougal's job have made his eyes sore as well? Comment on your answers.

3 In each case, what checks were there that the pieces which needed to be in line with the run of the material were correctly aligned? Comment on the reliablilty of these checks, particularly towards the end of a shift.

10.1 Electronic Control Systems

The control room of the ICI chemical plant which makes agricultural chemicals.

The Voyager 1 satellite near Saturn. Most of the control systems of the satellite operate automatically — signals from Earth take several minutes to reach it.

Computers are being installed to control a wide variety of equipment in factories. The computers **monitor** the equipment, decide what to do next, and send control signals. The overall steps of a control system are:

$$\text{Sense} \rightarrow \text{Decide} \rightarrow \text{Act.}$$

For example, in Figure 10.1, the sensors monitor the temperature and pressure of the chemical reaction. The computer uses the signals from the monitors to decide how to control the reaction. It sends control signals which open and close valves, and adjust the heating of the reaction.

Some computer-controlled machines are fully automatic. Others, like the fabric cutter in the story, are partly automatic. They all have one feature in common — they can be **programmed** to carry out a sequence of actions under the control of the computer. The person operating the machine can vary the program which the machine follows, but does not control its step-by-step operation.

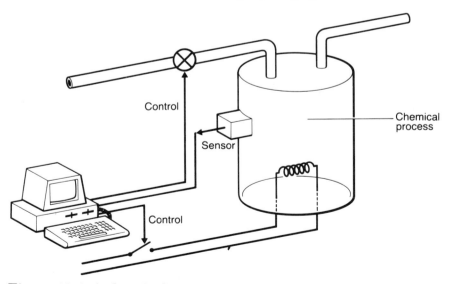

Figure 10.1: A chemical process monitored and controlled by computer

Many industrial processes are carried out under the control of computers. These include chemical processes (as shown in Figure 10.1), oil refining and the manufacture of glass. Similar computers are used in nuclear power stations to control the reactor. These computers monitor the process, and adjust the controls accordingly.

Motor vehicle manufacturers are installing **robots** to take over some assembly tasks from workers. The robots are programmed to carry out sequences of operations. They can lift objects, fasten them to other objects, weld, paint and test vehicles at various stages of assembly. The robots are controlled by small computers. These are in turn controlled by larger computers which co-ordinate the entire assembly process.

There are four main reasons for the rapid spread of computer-controlled machines and robots. They are **speed**, **flexibility**, **reliability** and **cost**.

- Most computer-controlled machines work more quickly than manually controlled ones. They produce more goods in the same time. They can respond rapidly to changing circumstances, and act quickly in an emergency.

- Computer-controlled machines and robots can do a wider range of tasks than the manually operated equipment they have replaced. It is easy to change them from one control program to another, so that they do a different task.

- Robots and machines controlled by computer are very reliable. If the operator of a manually controlled machine is tired, bored or feels ill, the quality of the work done on the machine suffers. Computers and robots do not get tired or bored, and they seldom break down.

- Automatically controlled machines and robots need fewer workers to run them. This saves money on wages. Large amounts of money are saved after a whole factory changes to computer-controlled equipment.

The main factor slowing down the introduction of robots and computer-controlled machines is the cost of purchasing the equipment. Robots and electronically controlled machines are very expensive, although their costs are gradually reducing.

QUESTIONS

1 a) List some tasks performed by robots in vehicle assembly plants.
   b) List some other tasks done by factory robots that you know of.

2 What are the **four** advantages of computer-controlled equipment? Can you think of any other advantages?

3 What are the overall steps of a control system?

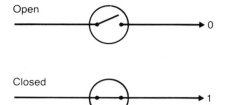

Figure 10.2: A control switch

10.2 Computer Logic

The simplest type of control is to switch something on, or switch it off. We do this all the time with lights, motor car engines, television sets, etc. The operation of a control switch of this type is shown in Figure 10.2. When it is **open** (or off), no control signal is sent. This is represented by a 0. When the switch is **closed** (or on), there is a control signal, shown as a 1.

The **control circuit** for a doorbell is shown in Figure 10.3. The switch is the button. This is connected to the doorbell. When the switch is closed, a signal is sent to the doorbell, which rings.

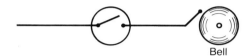

Figure 10.3: A doorbell

NOT Gate

Control signals are processed by **gates**. The simplest of these is a **NOT** gate, which reverses the signal. If it receives a 0 as input, it sends out a 1 as output, and vice versa (see Figure 10.4, and the table below).

Figure 10.4: A NOT gate

Figure 10.5 shows the control circuit for a light which comes on automatically when it is dark. The control switch is a light sensor. When it is light, the switch is closed, and when it is dark it is open. The signal from this switch is sent through a NOT gate to the light. When it is light, the switch sends out a 1. This is changed to a 0 by the NOT gate, and the light stays off. When it gets dark, the switch sends out a 0. This is changed to a 1 by the NOT gate, and the light comes on.

NOT Input	Output
0	1
1	0

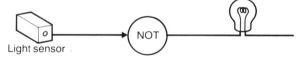

Figure 10.5: A light which comes on when it is dark

AND Gate

Two control signals may be combined by an AND gate. This sends out a 1 as output if it receives a 1 on the one input **and** a 1 on the other input. Otherwise it sends out a 0. (see Figure 10.6 and the table below).

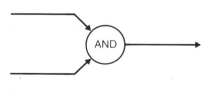

Figure 10.6: An AND gate

AND Inputs		Output
0	0	0
0	1	0
1	0	0
1	1	1

Figure 10.7 shows the control circuit for a warning light which flashes on and off when it is switched on. The one switch turns the light on. The other sends out a stream of pulses: 0, 1, 0, 1 etc. They are the inputs to an AND gate. The output from the gate is connected to the light.

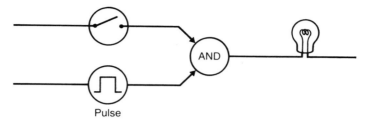

Figure 10.7: A warning light

Look at the table for the AND gate. The left input column is the switch, and the right input column is the pulse. When the switch is off (0), and the pulse is 0, the top row shows that the output is also 0. When the pulse changes to 1, the second row shows that the output stays 0. The light stays off while the switch is off.

When the switch is on (1), and the pulse is 0, the third row shows that the output is 0. When the pulse changes to 1, the output changes to 1, and the light comes on. The light flashes on and off while the switch is on.

OR Gate

Another common gate is the **OR** gate. This sends out a 1 if it receives a 1 on one input **or** a 1 on the other input. It also sends out a 1 if **both** inputs are 1 (see Figure 10.8 and the table below).

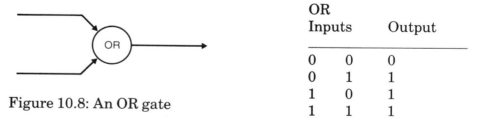

Figure 10.8: An OR gate

OR		
Inputs		Output
0	0	0
0	1	1
1	0	1
1	1	1

The combinations of Os and 1s produced by the gates are called **Boolean Logic**, after George Boole (1815 — 1864) who first investigated them. Boolean logic is the theory behind the way computers and control systems operate.

QUESTIONS

1 What does a NOT gate do to an input signal?

2 What inputs does an AND gate need to give a 1 output?

3 What inputs does an OR gate need to give a 0 output?

● ACTIVITY

10.3 Central Heating Control

The central heating system of a house is controlled automatically. When it is switched on, a **sensor** measures the temperature in the house. When this falls below a certain level, the heating comes on. When the temperature rises above this point again, the heating goes off.

- Design a control circuit for a central heating system of this sort. Use a heat sensor which sends out a 1 when the temperature is above a certain level, and a 0 when it is below this level. You will also need a switch to turn the system on and off, and two gates.

- Draw a diagram of the control circuit in a similar style to the others in this chapter.

  Follow combinations of 0s and 1s through your diagram, to see if it works correctly.

- Using an electronics kit, set up a circuit like the one you have designed. Connect the output to a light which comes on when the heating is on.

- Test your circuit. Use the heat from your finger to warm the heat sensor.

- Copy and complete the following table, showing how the central heating control system works.

Inputs		Output
Switch	Heat Sensor	Heater Control
0	0	
0	1	
1	0	
1	1	

QUESTIONS

1 What will happen if the central heating system is accidentally turned on during a hot day?

2 What will happen if the heat sensor is placed near a window, which is left open on a cool day?

● ACTIVITY

10.4 Burglar Alarm

A certain type of burglar alarm on a house is set off if a person walks through a light beam, or if they approach a window, where they are detected by their body heat. It also has a switch which allows it to be turned on or off.

- Design a circuit for this burglar alarm. You will need a switch to turn it on and off, a light sensor (0 if no light, 1 if there is light),

and a heat sensor (0 if no heat, 1 if there is heat). These are connected via three gates to a buzzer as output.

- Draw the circuit diagram for the burglar alarm, in the same style as those in the rest of this chapter.

  Follow combinations of 0s and 1s through the circuit, to check that it works properly.

- Using an electronics kit, set up this circuit and test it. Use the heat from your hand to activate the heat sensor.

- Copy and complete the following table, which shows how the burglar alarm works.

Inputs			Output
Switch	Light	Heat	Buzzer
0	0	0	
0	0	1	
0	1	0	
0	1	1	
1	0	0	
1	0	1	
1	1	0	
1	1	1	

- Modify the circuit to make the buzzer 'beep' on and off when the alarm goes off. You will need to include a pulse input and another gate. Draw a diagram for the modified circuit. Follow combinations of 0s and 1s through the circuit to check that it works properly.

QUESTIONS

1 What will happen if the alarm is switched on during the day, and the sun shines on the heat sensor?

2 What will happen if someone passes very quickly through the light beam? Suggest ways of modifying the alarm to solve this problem.

• A C T I V I T Y   10.5   Counter

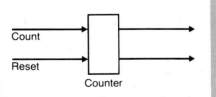

Count

Reset

Counter

Figure 10.9: Counter circuit

A **counter** is a circuit with a count input, a **reset** input and two or more outputs (see Figure 10.9). The pattern of 0s and 1s formed by the outputs is regarded as a **binary** (base two) number. For a counter with two outputs, the numbers are 0 0, 0 1, 1 0 and 1 1.

When a signal is received at the reset input, the output changes to 0 0. Each time a pulse reaches the count input, the output changes to the next binary number. For example, if the ouput is 0 1, a count changes it to 1 0. After 1 1, the output changes back to 0 0.

Figure 10.10 shows a circuit which counts every fourth pulse. The pulse generator is connected to the count input. The outputs are connected via an AND gate to a light. Every fourth pulse, when the output reaches 1 1, the AND gate outputs a 1. This switches on the light.

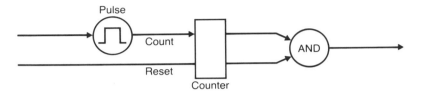

Figure 10.10: Circuit to count every fourth pulse.

- Connect up a circuit like the one in Figure 10.10. Check that it counts every fourth pulse.

When a beam of light is broken by an object passing it, a light sensor in the beam produces the sequence 1, 0, 1. If this is passed through a NOT gate, it becomes a pulse: 0, 1, 0.

- Use this information to modify the above circuit to count every fourth object passing through a light beam. Make a buzzer sound when this happens.

- Draw a circuit diagram of this counter, and set up a circuit to show how it works. Test it by moving your finger across the light sensor a number of times. Check that the buzzer sounds every fourth time.

Counters of this sort have many uses. They may be set to count every tenth or sixtieth pulse, and used in the displays of digital watches and clocks. Automatic counters are used on factory production lines.

QUESTIONS

1 Write down the sequence of outputs from a counter with three output lines.

2 Modify the circuit designed in this section to include a three-output counter, and count every eighth object. You will need an additional AND gate.

10.6 Programmable Control

Many simple control systems are wired up directly, using AND, OR and NOT gates, as described in the previous sections. More complex devices are controlled by **programs**. These are sequences of instructions which direct the step-by-step operation of the device. The program is either run by a computer, or by a **microprocessor** which is specially designed for the task.

Two robot trolleys which carry rolls of newsprint to newspaper presses. These are in use at the Manchester printing plant of the 'Daily Telegraph'.

The programs take inputs from control switches and sensors. They do calculations and make decisions based on the information from these inputs. They issue control signals accordingly. They have **loops**, which are repeated cycles of instructions.

Figure 10.11 shows the route of an automatic trolley which supplies three workstations in a factory. It starts at the stores, where it is loaded. It then moves from one workstation to the next, where items are removed. Each time the person at the workstation is finished with it, he or she presses a button which moves it on to the next workstation.

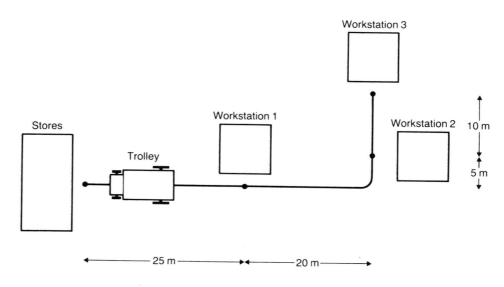

Figure 10.11: Factory trolley

The program which controls the trolley looks something like this. It starts with the trolley at the stores. (There is a comment in brackets next to each line. These are not part of the program.)

Repeat	(Repeat the following:-)
Get start-switch	(Wait for switch at Stores)
Right 180	(Turn around)
Forward 25	(Travel 25 metres)
Get start-switch	(Wait for switch at Station 1)
Forward 20	(Travel 20 metres)
Left 90	(Turn left)
Forward 5	(Travel 5 metres)
Get start-switch	(Wait for switch at Station 2)
Forward 10	(Travel 10 metres)
Get start-switch	(Wait for switch at Station 3)
Left 180	(Turn around)
Forward 15	(Travel 15 metres)
Right 90	(Turn right)
Forward 45	(Travel 45 metres)

The program is a loop which is repeated indefinitely. It takes the trolley from the stores, to each workstation and back again.

QUESTIONS

1 If the person at a workstation does not need the trolley, will it go past the workstation automatically?

2 a) Using a scale of 10cm to 1 metre, copy Figure 10.11 (in chalk) onto the floor of your classroom.
b) Write a program for your **Bigtrak** or programmable buggy so that it follows the motions of the factory trolley on the scale drawing.

3 Write a program to drive the trolley or your programmable buggy along the route shown in Figure 10.12.

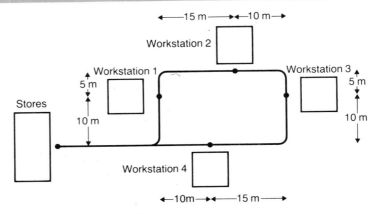

Figure 10.12: Revised trolley route

4 Draw a factory plan of your own, and design a trolley route for it. Write a program for the route, either for the trolley or for your programmable buggy.

10.7 Disco lights

Good discos have hundreds of lights! Many of them can move, and there is often a laser or two. The lasers can move, and be bounced off mirrors at various points in the disco. The lights are controlled by a computer. The computer enables the disk jockey to set up sequences of lighting displays which suit various records, and then call them up as the records are played. The lights can be synchronised with the music via sensors which can pick up different sounds, such as drum beats.

A simple disco light controller has eight control channels. Each switches on one bank of lights. It has a number of sensors, including one for the bass drum, one for cymbals, one for low notes and one for high notes.

A program for this disco light controller is as follows. It waits for the bass drum, and then switches on a sequence of lights.

```
Repeat                    (Repeat the following:-)
    Get bass-drum         (Wait for bass drumbeat)
    Put 1 0 0 0 0 0 0 0   (Switch on first light bank)
    Wait 10               (Pause 0.1 seconds)
    Put 0 0 1 0 0 0 0 0   (Switch on third light bank)
    Wait 10               (Pause 0.1 seconds)
    Put 0 0 0 0 1 0 0 0   (Switch on fifth light bank)
    Wait 10               (Pause 0.1 seconds)
    Put 0 0 0 0 0 0 1 0   (Switch on seventh light bank)
```

The Put command is followed by eight digits, one for each bank of lights. A zero means than the bank is off, a 1 means that it is on. The sequence 1 0 0 0 0 0 0 0 switches the first bank on, and all the rest off. (Some control systems use the word **output** or a similar word instead of **put** — see the instructions for your system.)

The Wait command is followed by a time in hundredths of a second.

- If you have a control system on your school's computer which has similar inputs and outputs, and a similar control language, translate the above program for this control system and enter it. Use a suitable sensor in place of the bass drum input.

- Run the program, and check that it produces the sequence of outputs that you would expect.

- Write a program, either using the above control language or the one for your own control system, for the following:

> Wait for the bass drum
> Flash the second bank of lights on and off twice
> Switch the fourth bank of lights on
> Wait for the cymbals
> Switch all the lights on

If possible, set up the control system on your school's computer to run this program.

- Devise other interesting lighting combinations of your own, and write programs for them.

QUESTIONS

1 How can the disco lights be synchronised with the music?

2 What are the limitations of the programs described in this section?

10.8 | Computer Elements: Microprocessor

In every computer and electronic control system there are one or more **microprocessor** chips. These are made from small pieces of silicon, approximately six millimetres square and one millimetre thick. On this are formed thousands of electrical circuits, which carry out logical operations as described in Section 10.2. The piece of silicon is mounted in a plastic carrier, with fine wires connecting it to the pins of the chip.

Microprocessor chips carry out programs, step by step. Each operation is done extremely quickly, in most cases by circuits within the chip. Information and instructions are fetched from separate **memory chips**. Information may also be transferred on input and output channels.

The advantages of microprocessors are that they are very fast, very reliable and very cheap. They use hardly any electricity, and do not generate much heat. They can be run non-stop for years without breaking down. If they do go wrong, they are simply unplugged and replaced.

The low cost and reliability of microprocessors have enabled the prices of computers to come down, while their processing power goes up. They are the main reason for the widespread introduction of robots and electronically controlled machines.

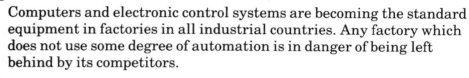

QUESTIONS

1 What are microprocessors made of?

2 What do microprocessors do?

3 Where do microprocesors get the programs and information they use?

4 Why are microprocessors becoming so popular?

10.9 Automatic Control in Practice

Computers and electronic control systems are becoming the standard equipment in factories in all industrial countries. Any factory which does not use some degree of automation is in danger of being left behind by its competitors.

The biggest users of robots and computerised equipment are motor vehicle manufacturers. Over the last ten years, assembly plants have been re-equipped or replaced entirely. The new plants use more automated equipment, and fewer workers. The change to automation was necessary because of rising costs and declining quality of vehicles. Most companies were making huge losses. Car firms in Europe and the USA were suffering from the competition from Japan. The introduction of electronic equipment, and the changes in work practices of the remaining workers, have helped bring motor manufacturers back into profit.

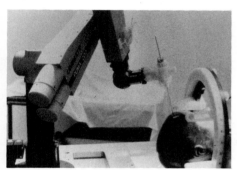

A robot which has been used to guide a probe to the precise location of a brain tumour during surgery.

The computer-controlled float glass production system in operation at Pilkington glassworks in St Helens.

Industrial processes such as oil and gas production, oil refining, steelmaking and chemical production have become increasingly automated in recent years. The change has not been as dramatic as in the motor industry, but the effects have been similar: lower costs, higher quality and fewer workers.

A bomb disposal robot
investigating a motor car in
New York.

A flight simulator used by
British Airways to train pilots
for the Boeing 757 aircraft.

Aircraft, missiles, tanks, ships and submarines are making
increasing use of on-board computers and electronic control systems.
Aircraft have automatic pilots and instrument landing systems.
Missiles have heat-seeking guidance systems. Bomb disposal units
use remote-controlled robots to investigate suspicious objects, and
dismantle them if necessary. Some motor cars have microprocessors
for certain controls.

In the home, microwave ovens, washing machines, sewing machines,
video recorders and television sets are incorporating
microprocessors. These enable the devices to be programmed, and left
to operate on their own.

The change to electronic control, by computers and microprocessors,
is by no means complete. Electronic control is likely to become even
more widespread than it is at present.

QUESTIONS

1 What were the reasons for introducing robots in car assembly
plants? What are the consequences of their introduction?

2 List some industrial processes which are controlled by
computer. Include those mentioned in the text, and others you
know of.

3 List some devices in the home which incorporate
microprocessors.

Exercise 10

1 Write down the meanings of the following words or phrases: sensor, program, robot, Boolean logic, control circuit, gate, sensor, counter, binary, microprocessor, loop, memory chip.

2 Draw control circuits for each of the following. Then set up the circuits and test them using an electronics kit. Draw up a table of the inputs and outputs of each one.

a) The control system of a refrigerator has a switch to turn the fridge on, and a heat sensor. If the fridge is on, and the temperature rises above a certain level, the motor is switched on. When the temperature falls below the set level, the motor is turned off.

b) An automatic door has a light beam on one side and a pressure mat on the other side. If someone breaks the light beam, or stands on the pressure mat, the door opens.

c) A factory robot which moves rolls of paper has two safety systems to stop it bumping into people. It has a heat sensor and a pressure switch on the front. If the heat sensor detects a person, or the switch is pressed, the robot stops. Design a control circuit which sends out a 1 if the robot can go, and a 0 if it must stop.

3 Program your **Bigtrak** or buggy to do some of the following. In each case, draw a suitable diagram on the floor for the vehicle to follow.
a) A supply vehicle which shuttles between two points, and pauses for a fixed length of time at each point.
b) A factory trolley which works as in Section 10.6, except that if no signal to proceed has been received after a suitable interval, it moves on by itself.
c) A supply vehicle which shuttles between four points, numbered 1 to 4. At each point it stops, and the number of the next point to which it must go is typed. It then travels to that point.

Things to Find Out

1 Select **one** of the industrial processes mentioned in Section 10.9. Find out:
a) How was the process carried out before computers and electronic control systems were introduced?
b) How is the process done using the electronic systems?
c) What effects has the change had, on the company, its workers and its customers?

Write a report on your findings, and give your opinion of the advantages and disadvantages of the changes.

2 Find out about uses of microprocessors in industry in addition to those described in this chapter.

3 **Music synthesisers** are instruments which can be programmed to play tunes. They can also produce a range of sounds which do not sound like any other instrument! Find out how they work, and how they are programmed. Also find out how they are used by bands when playing on stage, and making records.

If possible, write a program yourself to produce a tune or interesting sound.

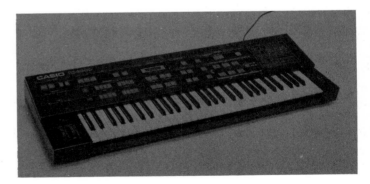

Points to Discuss

1 The most far-reaching effect of the introduction of electronic control systems has been a reduction in the number of jobs in many industries. In the motor industry in the UK, for example, this reduction has been approximately 50% between 1975 and 1985.

There are two sides to this issue. On the one hand, there is the hardship caused by mass unemployment. The job losses have affected some communities far more than others. In those badly affected, local businesses from building societies to fish and chip shops have also suffered, and many have closed down.

On the other hand, the products made with the new equipment are better and cheaper. The companies which make them are able to compete in world markets. The smaller number of jobs which remain are more secure, and the companies are making a valuable contribution to the economy as a whole. In many cases, the alternative to introducing new technology has been to close down altogether.

Discuss the various aspects of this situation, from the point of view of:

a) workers who have been made redundant, and their families;

b) workers who remain in the new factories;
c) Trade Unions which represent the workers;
d) managers of the factories;
e) people who buy the products;
f) the country as a whole.

One way of arranging this discussion is in the form of a debate, between pupils acting as Trade Union representatives and other pupils acting as managers. Speakers from the floor can play the roles of local businessmen, customers, local councillors, etc.

2 Another major effect of the introduction of automated equipment in factories is the need for re-training. Many traditional jobs are disappearing, and being replaced by new ones. Some of the new jobs require a higher level of skill than those which they are replacing, but this is not always the case. It is no longer true to assume that a person will stay in the same line of work throughout his or her career.

Discuss this situation, in particular the consequences it has for education at school and college.

Conclusion

● The directors of Marco Polo Tours are coming to the end of their meeting. At the meeting are Ronald McPerson (Managing Director), Jeremy Baldwin (Finance), Sandra Price (Marketing), Jonathan Saville (Operations) and Brian Hawkins (Computer Services).

Jeremy Baldwin: Last year's figures look good. We sold more holidays than ever before, and kept costs under control.

Ronald McPherson: What about our share of the market? Did we get a bigger percentage of the total than before?

Jonathan Saville: No — some of the new companies booked a lot of holidays. The total number of holidays is up, but our share of the total is down.

Ronald McPherson: Why?

Sandra Price: Part of the problem is marketing. We print brochures at the start of the season, and keep them the same for the next six months. Some of the new companies can vary their prices week by week, depending on their bookings. We can't do that.

Ronald McPherson: It seems that information is the key. Why isn't the right information getting through to marketing?

Brian Hawkins: We have three separate computer

systems. The Operations department has one for all the bookings, Finance has one for the accounts, and Marketing has its own system. There are no links between them.

Sandra Price: What we want is a daily update on bookings, so that we can see which tours still have vacancies. We also want a link to the finance computer system, so that we can work out the new prices.

Ronald McPherson: Brian, can we do this?

Brian Hawkins: Yes, but it will take time and cost money. I shall need to know pretty clearly what is wanted before I can give you dates and costs.

Ronald McPherson: Let's put a working group onto this. Brian - you and Sandra decide between you what you want. Include Jonathan in the meetings so that costs don't get

out of control. We need the linked computer system working in time for next season. Remember, it's the information that counts, not the technology. We want to be the best tour operator in the business, not the owners of the most expensive computer system.

QUESTIONS

1 How many computer systems does Marco Polo Tours have at present? What are they used for?

2 What is wrong with the computer systems as they are?

3 What solution is suggested for the problem?

4 What is likely to happen to Marco Polo Tours if they do not change their computer system soon?

11.1 Information Systems

An Apple Macintosh microcomputer, one of the first to use screen windows to show several programs at the same time.

The previous nine chapters of this book have described different types of **information systems**. In each chapter, computers, telecommunications or control systems are used to solve particular types of problems, and provide particular types of services.

The work of many organisations cannot be classified in one of these ways, as the story in the previous section illustrates. Companies need the right information in the right place at the right time. To achieve this, they often need direct links between all their computers, communications and control systems.

There are a number of ways of creating these combined information systems. If an organisation has all its information stored in a single, central **database**, then all the information systems it develops can be built up on this database. The organisation does, however, require a central computer system for the database.

Most large companies are based at a number of sites, often spread all over the world. They do not have a single central computer system, and many of their employees use desktop micros. These companies are installing **networks** to link all their computers, so that information can be sent rapidly to wherever it is needed.

Small organisations with a single desktop microcomputer have the same problem on a smaller scale. Many of them use word processing, spreadsheets and information retrieval software, as well as specialised programs. They need to be able to pass information between these systems. Some are beginning to use **integrated software** which combines word processing, spreadsheets and information retrieval. Others are using special software on their microcomputers which enables them to run more than one program at a time, and pass information between them.

Developing integrated computer systems is not easy. There are few common standards for sending and receiving information between different types of computer. It is even difficult to transfer information between microcomputers and mainframes made by the same manufacturer. Each type of computer program has its own way of storing information. Information needs to be translated from one representation to another in order to be passed across. In spite of these difficulties, linked IT systems within organisations, and direct links between the IT systems of different organisations are becoming increasingly common.

In all cases, the reasons for linking up the computer systems are the same. People need information to help them make decisions, solve problems and work effectively. IT is there to supply this information, to store it, process it and communicate it. Computer systems must be designed to meet the needs of their users. Users must not spend a lot of their valuable time meeting the needs of their computers.

QUESTIONS

1 List **four** ways in which separate computer systems are being combined.

2 Why are separate computer systems being linked or combined in many organisations?

3 What are the difficulties in linking computer systems together?

4 Are integrated information systems very rare?

● **ACTIVITY**   **11.2** **Get IT Together!**

In this activity you will create a table of figures using a spreadsheet, and copy it into a word processor document to form part of a report.

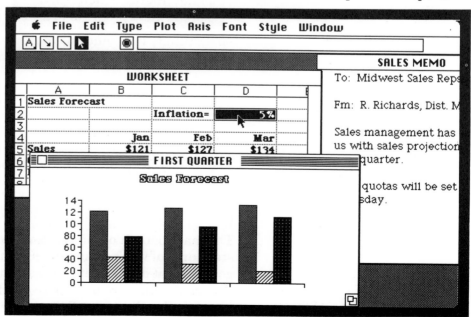

Three windows on a computer screen, showing a graph, a spreadsheet and a word processor document.

You will need either a linked set of software which is able to transfer information, or a program such as **MS Windows** which can run a spreadsheet and word processor at the same time.

Imagine that you are the Finance Director of Marco Polo Tours:

- Set up a spreadsheet showing the number of holidays sold, and the income and expenditure for each of the previous six months. See Chapter 4 for the method.

  Use headings as follows:

Month	No. of Hols	Income	Costs	Profit
April				
May				
June				
July				
August				
Sept				

- Save your spreadsheet on disk.

- Open up a word processor document for your report to the other directors. Write a brief report, giving reasons for the main trends in the figures.

- Copy the table of figures from the spreadsheet program into the word processor document. See the instructions for your programs for the method of doing this.

- Save the combined document on disk, and print it.

QUESTIONS

1 What are the benefits of being able to copy a table from a spreadsheet program to a word processor document?

2 Estimate how much of your time was saved by copying the table directly.

11.3 The Impact of IT

The social effects of the introduction of information technology have been discussed at a number of places in this book. The most important ones are the effects of IT on jobs, and problems when personal information is stored on computers.

The main benefit of information technology is an improvement in standards of work. Companies, banks, hospitals, police forces, and government departments are able to provide better services. Social Security claims are paid more quickly. The collection of taxes, VAT in particular, is more efficient. The telephone service in Britain and

many other countries has improved a great deal as new equipment has been installed.

With higher standards have come lower costs. A number of large companies, especially motor manufacturers and steelworks, would have gone out of business if they had not introduced new technology. Lower costs have also meant lower rates and taxes for government services.

These trends are likely to continue for some time. Information technology is used extensively at present, but there is scope for much greater use. Within the EEC, countries such as Greece, Spain and Portugal are a long way behind Britain, France and West Germany in their use of IT. Many developing countries are using information technology in only a very limited way. They are unlikely to reach the levels of use of the leading Western nations, but some increase in their use of IT will bring great benefits.

Information technology is there to help. It takes over routine aspects of work, and enables people to do the important jobs more effectively. It provides new opportunities, and new challenges. It is essential to know what information technology can do, and to be familiar with its use.

QUESTIONS

1 a) What are the main benefits of the use of information technology?
b) What are the main problems?

2 Which are the leading European countries in the use of IT?

3 Is information technology used much in the Third World at present? How is this situation likely to change?

Comment on your answers.

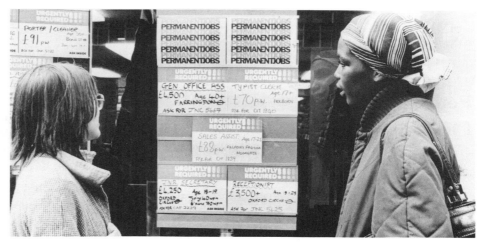

Exercise 11

1 Put yourself in the place of Brian Hawkins, in the story at the start of this chapter.
a) Write a brief description of the links needed for the three computer systems at Marco Polo Tours.
b) State clearly the purposes of these links.
c) Describe how the new marketing system will operate.

2 Why is information so important in a company like Marco Polo Tours?

3 Information can usefully be transferred from a number of software packages into reports prepared on a word processor. Some suggestions are as follows:

a) Tables of numbers or graphs prepared as part of the wildlife or weather surveys described in previous chapters can be copied directly into reports on these surveys.

b) A report on a chess match can include a diagram of the board, prepared on a CAD program.

c) Stories written using a word processor can include illustrations from a drafting program. An idea for a class project is a series of children's stories on a particular theme, written and illustrated by members of the class.

Things to Find Out

1 Carry out a survey of the knowledge of, and attitudes towards information technology. Either survey other pupils, teachers or parents. This can be done as a group or class project.

a) Design the survey very carefully. As far as possible, ask questions which can be answered with 'Yes', 'No' or 'Don't Know'.
  For example, you might wish to include a section on word processing. The questions might look something like this:

1 Have you ever used a word processor:
   at work?   Yes/No
   at home?   Yes/No

2 Can a word processor be used to:
   type letters?   Yes/No/Don't Know
   do calculations?   Yes/No/Don't Know

3 Would you prefer to use a word processor rather than an electric typewriter?
                               Yes/No/Don't Know

The second question is designed to see how much people know about word processing.

b) When you have decided what questions to ask, type them carefully into a word processor document. Set them out neatly, and make sure that they are easy to read.
Print the questions, and make a set of copies of them.

c) Either let the people being surveyed fill in the question sheets themselves, or ask them the questions, and write down their answers.

d) Use a spreadsheet or statistical program to enter and analyse the results. Draw graphs, bar charts or pie charts of the results where appropriate.

e) Discuss the results, and think about them carefully. Suggest reasons for any trends you observe.

f) Write a report on the results of the survey. Do it on a word processor, and include tables, graphs or pie charts from the program that has analysed the results.

2 Look for articles in local newspapers which report on the introduction of information technology in your area. Read the articles carefully, and decide:
a) how much the reporters know about information technology;
b) how much the readers are expected to know about IT.

Comment on your conclusions.

Points to Discuss

1 Look at the shops, businesses and community services in your area. Discuss the overall contribution made by information technology to these organisations. Has IT brought about an improvement in standards? What adverse effects has the introduction of IT had?

2 Discuss ways in which an increased use of information technology could affect your community. Consider the issues which have been raised in this book — employment, unemployment, privacy of personal information, standards of service and prices.

This discussion can be arranged as a debate between those who favour an increase in the use of new technology, and those who would prefer it not to be used. Each side could prepare posters and slogans to support their case.

Glossary of Terms

analogue a signal where the strength of the signal is proportional to the quantity it represents.

automatic test equipment equipment which is controlled by a computer or microprocessor and which tests manufactured goods.

banker's draft an instruction from a bank to transfer a sum of money from one of its accounts to an account at another bank.

bar code a pattern of wide and narrow stripes which encodes a number.

binary numbers in base two.

Boolean logic the theory behind the way microprocessors work.

card index a simple file on a set of cards.

cash terminal a terminal used by banks for dispensing money.

cell a place in a computer memory for one item of information.

check digit an extra digit on a number for checking purposes.

chip a small, solid state device which stores or processes information.

computer a digital, electronic information processing machine.

computer-aided design (CAD) the use of computers to design things.

control circuit a circuit which shows how a set of control switches and gates are linked.

control unit the part of a computer which controls its step-by-step operation.

counter an electronic circuit which counts.

cursor the highlighted area on a computer or word processor screen which indicates where the next character is to be typed.

database a large store of related information which can be used for a number of purposes.

database system a computer system which manages a database.

digital information stored or signals sent as a sequence of digits.

digital plotter an output device which draws pictures or plans.

digital telephone exchange a telephone exchange which handles calls and computer messages in digital form.

digitising pad an input device for drawing pictures onto a computer screen.

disk a disk which stores information as patterns of magnetised spots.

disk drive a backing store device which transfers information to and from a disk.

disk pack a set of disks mounted on the same shaft.

display screen an output device like a television screen, on which information is displayed.

document a letter or similar file of text used by a word processing system.

draft copy an early version of a letter or other document.

electronic funds transfer the transfer of money between banks by a direct computer link.

electronic mail the transfer of documents or files between computers via a telecommunications link.

elevation a drawing of a building viewed from the side, front or rear.

fibre optics a cable made of thin strands of glass which carries signals as pulses of light.

field the place for one item of information in a record.

file a structured set of information, consisting of a set of records.

foreign correspondent a person who is sent to a foreign country to send back reports to a newspaper.

gate a device which processes one or more signals.

gateway a route from a viewdata system to another computer system.

graphics the use of computers to produce pictures or draw graphs.

hard copy printed output from a computer.

hire purchase buying something and paying for it by instalments.

information provider a person or company who supplies information for a viewdata system.

information retrieval system a computer system which stores information and allows it to be retrieved.

information technology the combination of computers, communications and control systems, all based on microchips.

input to get information into a computer.

invoice a document which shows how much must be paid for something.

keyboard the set of keys on which input information can be typed into a computer or word processor.

light pen a pen which enables lines to be drawn on the display screen of a computer.

local area network a network linking computers and other devices in the same building.

local viewdata service a viewdata service covering a restricted area.

loop a part of a program which is repeated.

mailbox the place for receiving messages on an electronic mail or viewdata service.

memory the part of a computer which stores the information and programs which are in use at the time.

memory chip a chip which stores information and programs.

message switching computer a computer in a communications network which switches messages from their senders to their receivers.

microchip see **chip**.

microprocessor a chip which processes information.

minimum stock level the stock level at which an order for more stock is placed.

modem a device which connects a computer to a telephone line.

monitor (1) the display screen on a computer.
　　　　　(2) to take continuous measurements of the operation of a process.

movement record the record of stock coming into or out of a shop or warehouse.

multiplexer a device which connects a number of telephone lines into a computer.

output to get information out of a computer.

page a screenful of information on a viewdata system.

perspective view a drawing of a building viewed from an angle, with the distant parts smaller than the closer parts.

plan a drawing of a building as seen from above.

portfolio a collection of shares in companies.

printed circuit board (PCB) a fibreglass board on which are mounted chips and other components.

printout printed output from a computer.

processor the part of a computer where information is processed.

program a set of instructions which control the operation of a computer or control system.

random access memory (RAM) memory chips on which any information can be stored and read back.

read-only memory (ROM) memory chips on which the information and programs are stored permanently.

record a set of items of information in a file.

reference the name given to a document on a word processing system.

re-order quantity the amount of stock to be ordered when it falls below the minimum stock level.

response frame a viewdata page on which a user can order goods, book tickets or ask for more information.

robot a device which is programmed to carry out certain manual tasks.

sample a number representing a portion of a continuous signal.

sensor a device which measures temperature, light, pressure, etc.

silicon disk a portion of a computer menory which is used as if it were a disk.

solid-state describes a device such as a microchip, which has no moving parts.

spreadsheet a table of numbers and other information which can be manipulated by a computer.

telecommunications a network of communications links for telephone calls, computer messages, telex messages, etc.

terminal a device which provides a direct link between a computer and a person using it.

top copy the final copy of a letter or document.

trunk line a telephone line between two exchanges.

viewdata a computer system which enables users to see a large collection of pages of information.

Winchester disk a small, high-capacity magnetic disk.

word processor a computer used to type, edit, store, retrieve and print documents.

Index

Acknowledgements

The author and publishers are grateful to the following for permission to use their photographs:

Michael Aaron: *125*;   Acorn: *12* (top), *20* (top), *51* (top);   All Sport: *18*;   Amstrad: *25*;   Apple: *134, 135*;
Art Directors: *57* (top);   British Telecom: *112* (bottom);   Canon: *21*;   Casio: *131*;   Computer Vision: *80*;
Donald Cooper: *84*;   Daily Telegraph: *88*;   Eastman Co: *116*;   Educational Electronics: *68, 74* (top);   EMI: *58* (right);
Format: *137* (bottom);   General Practitioner Magazine: *42*;   Hewlett Packard: *86*;   IBM: *22* (top), *87*;
ICI: *118* (top);   ICL: *12* (bottom), *39* (bottom), *112* (top), *128*;   Infopress: *31*;   John Lewis: *63* (bottom);
Lloyds: *113*;   Meteorological Office: *71*;   Metropolitan Police: *40, 41*;   Pilkington: *129* (bottom);   Plessey: *20* (bottom);
Post Office: *44*;   Potterton: *122*;   Rex: *8* (left); *9, 10* (top), *12* (bottom), *94, 110, 123, 129* (top), *130* (top), *137* (top);
RSPB: *37*;   Science Photo Library: *16, 30, 64, 99, 100, 107, 118* (bottom);   SIPA-Press: *49*;
Smith Industries: *75* (bottom);   Thomson Holidays: *92*;   Times Books: *109*;   Vickers Medical: *75* (top);
Wrangler: *117*;   Zefa: *8* (top, bottom)

The publishers have made every effort to trace the relevant copyright holders, but if they have inadvertently omitted any appropriate acknowledgements they will be pleased to make suitable corrections at the earliest opportunity.

143